HOKKAIDO

OTARU
ASAHIKAWA
L. TOYA
SAPPORO
MT. DAISETSU
L. AKAN
NOBORIBETSU
HAKODATE
KUSHIRO

EA

AOMORI
L. TOWADA
AKITA
MORIOKA
YAMAGATA
MATSUSHIMA
NIIGATA
SENDAI
FUKUSHIMA

AMA

ONSHU
NIKKO
GANO
KOFU
ONE
TOKYO
AMI
YOKOHAMA
KAMAKURA

PACIFIC OCEAN

JAPAN ALL-AROUND

MIURA PRINTING CORPORATION

Edited and Printed by
MIURA PRINTING CORPORATION,
Producer: Hisashi Miura
9-3, 2-chome, Chitose, Sumida, Tokyo 130, Japan
Published by
TOKYO SEVEN CORPORATION,
Miura Printing Bldg., 9-3, 2-chome, Chitose,
Sumida, Tokyo 130, Japan

JAPAN ALL-AROUND

Distributed by
JAPAN PUBLICATIONS TRADING CO., LTD.
P.O. Box 5030, Tokyo International,
Tokyo 100-31, Japan
2-1, Sarugaku-cho, 1-chome, Chiyoda-ku,
Tokyo 101, Japan
I.S.B.N. 0-87040-347-8

INTRODUCTION

If figures are used, among other means, to show any country as it is, then those showing Japan as it stands today run as follows:

I.   Area: 377,708 sq. km.
      Formed of the four main islands of Honshu or Main Island, Hokkaido, Kyushu, Shikoku, and Okinawa the country is equal in area to the State of Montana, U.S.A.

II.   Population: 117,060,396 (1980)
      314 people in 1 sq. km.
      About 1,900,000 more women.
      By 2000 A. D., the population is estimated to reach 128 million.

III. The best three of export (1981); (in $1,000)
      Automobile: 26,521,409
      Steel: 16,668,870
      Vessel: 7,273,622

In such figures, however, it is impossible to explain the Japanese way of thinking. Therefore, this book has provided, among those on the local features, chapters on the customs and manners, the history, the ways of living, etc., to explain as fully as possible the character of the Japanese people.

A unique culture has been established in Japan mainly because of its long history and its geographical distance from every continent of the world, but the twentieth century has seen the world become smaller and smaller, and the relations between Japan and other nations closer and closer. It is to be hoped that this volume will give a truer picture of the real Japan as it progresses.

CONTENTS

GENERAL

INTRODUCTION 3

LIFE IN NATURE AND NATURE IN LIFE 8

CLIMATE—The Four Seasons 21

CUSTOMS AND MANNERS 78

GEOGRAPHY 92

ARTS IN LIFE 98

RELIGION 112

ZEN 134

TRADITIONAL AMUSEMENTS 146

A SHORT VIEW OF LONG HISTORY 179
WITH A CHRONOLOGICAL TABLE

THE ECONOMY AND INDUSTRY OF JAPAN 213

NEW JAPAN 227

Everyday Life: Food, Clothing, etc. 229
Sports 234
Political System 237
Education 237

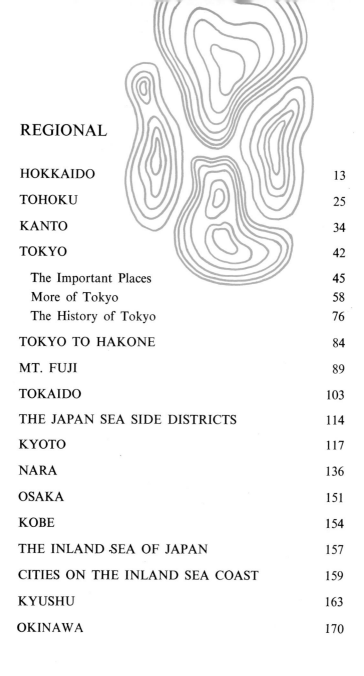

REGIONAL

HOKKAIDO   13

TOHOKU   25

KANTO   34

TOKYO   42

  The Important Places   45
  More of Tokyo   58
  The History of Tokyo   76

TOKYO TO HAKONE   84

MT. FUJI   89

TOKAIDO   103

THE JAPAN SEA SIDE DISTRICTS   114

KYOTO   117

NARA   136

OSAKA   151

KOBE   154

THE INLAND SEA OF JAPAN   157

CITIES ON THE INLAND SEA COAST   159

KYUSHU   163

OKINAWA   170

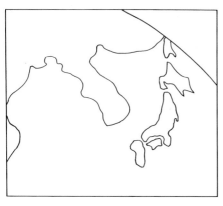

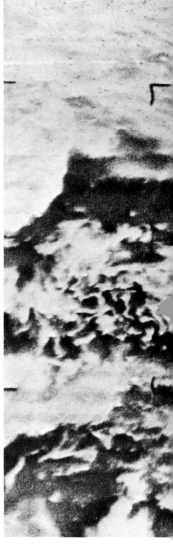

Japan Islands photographed by Tiros VIII, an American meteorological satellite.

LIFE IN NATURE AND NATURE IN LIFE

The climate exercises a great influence upon any culture in any part of the world. You cannot ignore this fact when you talk about the culture of Japan. While Japan is a small country, it creates a great diversity of climatic conditions, as is explained later in the sections on climate and topography. So Japan is exposed to natural disasters as often as it enjoys natural blessings.

No other country has more distinct changes of seasons than Japan. The seasons do not change so suddenly in Japan as they do from the wet to the dry in the tropics, but there is a spell of weather so mild, between the hot and cold seasons, that you feel like wearing clothes specially made for it.

It is man's dwelling that is most influenced by climate. All houses in Japan were made of wood until Western-style buildings and houses appeared. The houses made of wood are especially suitable for spending the hot and humid summer comfortably, though, of course, they cannot resist fire and wind. Although there is almost no house found today which is purely wooden, many are still predominantly made of wood. In a word, the traditional Japanese house, while serving as a place to keep men safe from the tyranny of nature, is intended for a life which is destined to make the most of the good in nature.

You may regard the Japanese garden as a medium to strengthen the contact of life with nature. Japanese gardening differs a great deal from that of Europe and America. The Japanese garden, once it is made, must become 'nature' itself, although it is first laid out by human hands and will. Or rather, it must embody an idea of nature as it should be. To each material used in Japanese gardening, such as water, stone, and trees, is given a meaning essential to its existence. In ancient Japan the garden was a scenic copy of the sea. In the Middle Ages (the Kamakura and Muromachi periods), which saw the highest art of gardening, attempts were made to represent, in a space of one square yard, the entire universe.

8

Water is an important element of a Japanese garden.
You will see a pond in Katsura Imperial Villa, Kyoto.
Before the circular gardening was completed, people
enjoyed seeing the garden-plot by boat.

The architecture of Katsura is typical *sukiya-zukuri*,
originated from the tea pavilion, simple and neat
in contrast with *shoin-zukuri* of aristocratic residen-
ces. Both styles have brought about today's typical
Japanese dwellings.

9

Striped fields of Uwajima, Shikoku, along the Seto Inland Sea.

It is certainly true that, as for clothing, what is traditional has almost completely disappeared from our daily living; but even now many of us are in the habit of wearing *kimono* after we have worked in European-style clothes. This shows that we do not forget to make our traditional and modern-style clothes go well together in our living, knowing that the *kimono* is superior to other forms of clothing in giving no artificial feeling as it covers the body comfortably.

Our staple food is rice. Statistics show that the Japanese ate 13,233,000 tons of crop in 1981, consuming in addition 1,737,000 tons of eggs, and 2,664,000 tons of meat. To our diversified climate we owe the various kinds of food that add pleasure to the table. And the variety of the Japanese dishes is not unrelated, in a way, to the habit of eating many things uncooked.

Thus the Japanese not only receive from nature what good it bestows upon them, but also cast their own thought back on nature. They appreciate the natural texture of a plain-wood pillar, whereas they enjoy painting the night sky with colourful man-made fireworks.

It is certainly true that the rapid inflow into Japan of foreign cultures since the nineteenth century has greatly transformed the traditional Japanese view of nature. In fact, in big cities today you will hardly find a single space over which nature holds sway. But, even those who are forced to live in standardized mammoth apartments of reinforced concrete never forget to wear *yukata* after taking a bath, and to hang *furin* (a wind-bell) at the window to hear it tinkle. *Yukata,* not a bathrobe, is the kind of light clothing in which a man can feel a touch of nature on the skin. The *furin* is just a sort of ornament which makes a tinkling sound in the smallest stream of air, but we enjoy the coolness in the metallic sound it tinkles forth in the cool wind.

The Japanese feel attached to spring and autumn far more than to summer or winter. Spring and autumn, the seasons neither too hot nor too cold, foster the sense of Japanese beauty.

These mild seasons mitigate for us the severity of nature. But even the severity of nature can sometimes co-exist with beauty. People travelling along the coast of the Inland Sea of Japan, one of the most beautiful spots in the world, will see some small islands cultivated almost all over, even to their tops. It is the fields beautifully arranged in regular tiers that are seen. These fields are the new forms of beauty produced in nature by the people who have labored to conquer the scarcity of arable land.

Typical residence of Japan's middle-class.

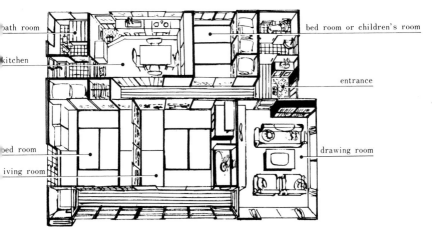

bath room

kitchen

bed room or children's room

entrance

bed room

living room

drawing room

Fireworks in Japan have been skillfully
developed. Star-like clusters spread
through the sky changing their colors
one by one. (at Atami City)

HOKKAIDO

Hokkaido is a large island, quadrilateral in shape, situated in the north of Japan. It is 30,304 square miles in area, occupying 21.2 per cent of the total area of Japan. It is twice as large as Denmark or Switzerland. Latitudinally, Hakodate, the southernmost city, lies somewhat higher than New York City, and the northern tip far lower than Paris. There is a strait separating Hokkaido from Honshu, and it takes about four hours to cross it on a ferryboat. The pilot tunnel has already been built under the strait. It is expected to be completed by 1987.

Located about one hour by air from Tokyo, Hokkaido presents natural features and ways of living quite different from those in Honshu. The land is flat and rich, and is ideal for farming and cattle breeding, which are prospering there. 727,000 tons

Lake
Mashu.

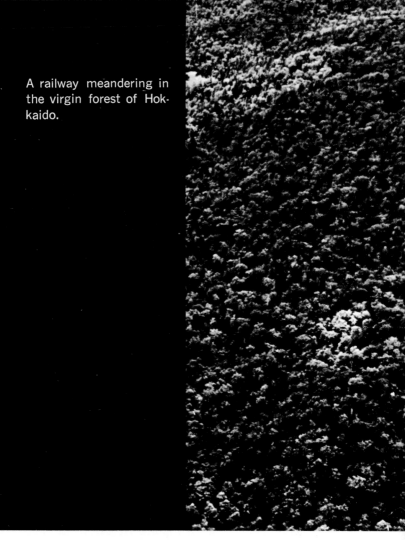

A railway meandering in the virgin forest of Hokkaido.

of rice was produced in 1982, an output surpassed only by that of Niigata Prefecture. The fishing industry is also prospering because of the island's long coast line, which represents 25 per cent of Japan's total coast lines. Hokkaido is also the central base of Japan's fishing operations in the north seas.

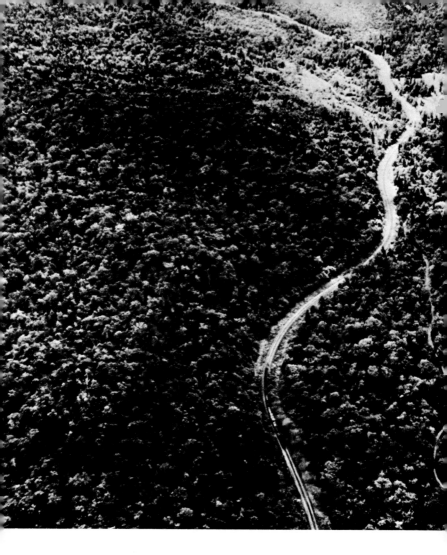

In Hokkaido there is no rainy season, the most unpleasant period in other parts of Japan. There is, however, much snowfall from October to April, even in the flat areas.

The summer is cool and beautiful, and thousands of people visit this island. For, to the Japanese, Hokkaido has always been "a land of dreams."

It was in 1869 that the full-scale development of this land was first undertaken under the direction of the government, and so, roughly speaking, the land is only one hundred years old.

For developing the land for the first time, many specialists were invited from abroad, and various new innovations were made. They divided the towns and cities into blocks, and built straight streets. They also adopted an extensive farming system.

Many of the towns are divided into blocks by straight roads, but the most beautiful must be the City of Sapporo. "Sapporo" means "a large dry place" in Ainu, the language of the natives of Hokkido, and it is natural that the streets of Sapporo are popularly called "parks," for they are more than 300 feet in width. In 1972 the 11th Sapporo Winter Season Olympic was held with 1,274 players participating from 35 countries.

Westminster Abbey, sphinx and pyramid, the Statue of Liberty and many famous structures made of snow and ice appear on the streets of Sapporo at the Snow Festival.

Settlers from overseas also spread the seeds of a new religion all over the island. It was by the teaching of Dr. Clark, for instance, that such eminent Japanese Christians as Inazo Nitobe and Kanzo Uchimura were first brought into contact with Christianity.

Ice chunks drifting from the Okhotsk Sea.

In its natural scenery, again, Hokkaido is distinct from the other islands of Japan. In the middle of the island rise the ranges of Mt. Daisetsu, surrounded on both sides by immense virgin forests, which form the greatest national mountainside park of Japan, with Mt. Asahi as its central feature. To the east of Mt. Asahi are such beautiful lakes as Kutcharo, Akan and Mashu. Lake Mashu, among others, charms the visitors with its mysterious scenery. There is no river flowing into or out of this lake. It is wrapped in mist almost all the year round.

Many lakes and swamps are also seen in the southern parts of Hokkaido, but those areas are more noted for their hot springs. There are some hotels which have no less than twenty-five large baths, all with different kinds of water.

The coast running from the Headland of Soya to the Headland of Shiretoko is closed in winter because it is invaded by masses of floating ice in the Sea of Okhotsk. Seals and other polar animals are often seen there.

*　　　　*　　　　*

The Name of the Country

The Japanese call their country *Nihon* or *Nippon*. In the olden days they used to call it *Ooyashima, Toyoashihara-Mizuhonokuni* or *Yamato*. The country began to be called by the present name in about 701 A. D. *Nihon* or *Nippon* (日本) means 'the origin of the sunrise'. It was born from the fact that the country is situated to the east of the Asian Continent and the sun rises in the east.

CLIMATE · The Four Seasons

Japan is subject to frequent climatic changes because, extending from north to south, it is surrounded by the sea on all sides and has complicated geographical features. Especially characteristic of the climate is the changing of the seasons that occurs almost exactly every three months. Except in the northern and southern extremities, spring comes in March, followed by the rainy season that sets in June, bringing summer, and in September the continental high atmospheric pressure brings the cool autumn. Towards the end of November the dry cold wind begins to blow, and it is winter. This is roughly the annual cycle of nature in our country.

From late February to early March, the drifts of high and low pressures frequently come over Japan, and mild fine days alternate with cold windy days. About this time of the year, the thaw sets in, and cherry blossoms and many other flowers begin to color first the southern and then the northern parts of Japan. People start working in accordance with this awakening of nature. All schools have commencement exercises in March, and new pupils in April. It is in April, too, that private companies and government offices enter a new fiscal year.

The rainy season comes between spring and summer and lasts about a month. It is brought about by unstable atomospheric conditions. Tropical heavy damp air masses keep flowing into the trough that the Okhotsk and the North Pacific high pressures create over Japan in June. This wet season usually has a favorable influence upon Japan's agriculture and water power generation. But when it turns out short or dry, we suffer from crop failures.

In summer the temperature usually rises to 79°F in and near Tokyo. It is only four or five degrees higher than in New York and Rome, but Tokyo seems much hotter because of its high humidity.

Floral fields.

Enjoying toy fire-joss-sticks in summer.

The hills surrounding Lake Towada, aflame with autumnal tints.

Midwinter in Hokuriku district on the Japan Sea Coast.

23

By the time summer is over, notorious typhoons come up north one after another to attack our country. The typhoons are born on the tropical seas near the equator, but influenced by the rotation of the earth, they go up north, following a course from the Philippines to Japan. While they are an annual threat to Japan, the enormous quantity of rain they bring is welcomed as an indispensable resource for our water power generation. So, every year we await the season of typhoons with mixed feelings.

In autumn the sky above Japan is cloudless and blue, and looks deeper. We welcome autumn, saying, "Autumn with the sky clear and blue, and horses going stout." A month or two in the wake of the typhoon season is for us one of the most comfortable periods of the year. In the paddy fields rice plants wave their golden heads, and the trees put on red leaves. The autumnal colors in Japan are varied and numerous, and are a grand spectacle of a different kind from those of Canada, which are one immense expanse of red leaves.

The cold seasonal wind blowing from Siberia brings winter into Japan. In winter most places of Japan may be a little warmer than, say, New York or Chicago. In January the temperature is usually 37°F in and near Tokyo, and in Chicago it is 25°F. In Sapporo, Hokkaido, the lowest temperature ever recorded is twenty degrees below zero, but, generally, the winter is easier for us to bear than the summer. We have a lot of snow in Japan in spite of its favorable latitudes. There is more snowfall on the coast of the Japan Sea because of the ranges of mountains rising in the central parts of Japan to check the spread of cold air blowing in from the Asian Continent. It doesn't snow very much in Tokyo and Osaka, but, as you see in the photograph, in some areas of the Tohoku and Hokuriku districts people are compelled to spend a greater part of the winter under snow.

TOHOKU

The Tohoku district consists of 6 prefectures. On June 23, 1982, Tohoku New Trunk Line (Omiya – Morioka; about 4 hours, 466 km) opened, followed by Joetsu New Trunk Line (Omiya – Niigata; about 2.5 hours, 270 km) that opened on November 15, 1982. Situated in northern Japan, the Tohoku district has the coldest winter next to Hokkaido, the average winter temperature ranging from 41°F to 23°F.

Compared with its large area, the Tohoku district is not blessed with much arable land, with the Ou mountain range extending from north to south halfway between the Japan Sea coast and the Pacific, and with the Kitakami mountains on the Pacific coast and the Dewa mountains on the Japan Sea side. But the plains of Akita, Shonai, Noshiro and Tsugaru are important granaries of Japan. The mountainous areas are rich in forest resources, orchard and dairy products.

In this part of Japan people give the name *Kaza-hana* ('wind-blossom') to the snow that falls in early November, regarding it as the harbinger of winter. Seeing the 'wind-blossom', they start to provide food and fuel for the long winter. The snow covers the cities as well as the fields and mountains. The grown-ups are prevented from working outdoors, so they make preparations for the spring, or make industrial art objects with wood and straw. Children in Akita Prefecture build a 'cave' of snow called *Kamakura,* which looks like the Eskimos' house of ice. Before television became popular, the fireplace (made in the floor) was for the children a pleasant place for relaxation in winter. They would sit around the fireplace and manage somehow or other to persuade their grandfathers to tell them an old tale told over many generations. Old folk stories are a valuable asset to the children's literature of Japan.

It was Minamoto-no Yoritomo, with his Bakufu (Shogunate government) established at Kamakura in 1185, that ruled this district, for the first time, as far as its northern tip, Aomori. Since then, the Tohoku district has been developed for agriculture and has come to support the economy of Japan as an important rice granary.

TOHOKU

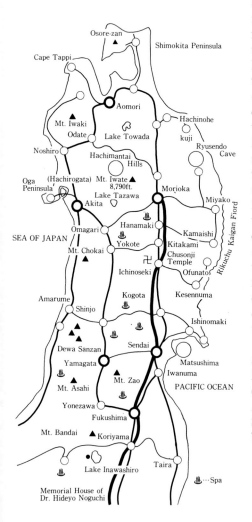

Tanabata

The *Tanabata* Festival comes from ancient Chinese myths. It is said to have been first introduced into Japan in the 7th century. There is a legend attached to the festival that Altair as a cowboy (star of the first magnitude in the constellation Aquilla) and the weaving girl or Vega (a brilliant white star in the constellation Lyra) meet across the Milky Way once a year on the night of July 7. People hang colored pieces of paperwork on fresh bamboo branches and put them up just outside the door. It is said that young women and children can have their wishes come true if they write them on cards and hang them on the bamboo branches. Today *Tanabata* festivals are held all over Japan on July 7, or in some districts on August 7 (July 7 in the lunar calendar). Among them, the festival at Sendai is the largest and most beautiful.

Tanabata, the Star Festival.

Towada-Hachimantai National Park

This National Park includes Lake Towada and its neighboring areas stretching over Aomori and Akita prefectures, and the Hachimantai area on the borders of Akita and Iwate Prefectures. Lake Towada is filled with clear water peculiar to north Japan, and is famous for trout cultivation. The Oirase River, flowing out of this lake, looks especially beautiful about the time the leaves turn red.

In the Hachimantai area there are many openings in the ground from which hot water boils out or gas blows out, signs of volcanic activities in the earth. Unforgettable are the alpine flowers and mysterious Lake Tazawa.

Shimokita Peninsula

This is the peninsula that sticks out like an ax from Aomori toward Hokkaido. In the middle of the ax-head there is a bleak rocky mountain called Osore-zan (literally 'The Dreadful Mountain') and Lake Usorizan. The northern shore of the lake looks hellish, for there is nothing but countless fumaroles and geysers making strange sounds, without a single speck of grass.

The attraction of the festival held on the mountain every year from July 21 to 24 is a blind female medium of primitive shamanism called *Itako*. People ask her to summon up the spirits of their departed relatives They console themselves by hearing the spirits speak. In this way they try to unload the weights of sadness that have accumulated during the past year.

In the famous Nebuta Festival at Aomori (Aug. 3 to 7) people parade through the streets at night, carrying huge *papier-maché* dolls with burning candles in them.

Among others, Hachinohe City is famous for its *Emburi* (Feb. 17 to 20) and Koma Folk Dance.

The Shonai Plain

This is the drainage basin of the Mogami River flowing into the Sea of Japan, and presents scenes of the traditional village life. In the snow, the Mogami River puts on an atmosphere of *Sansui-ga* (Japanese landscape painting).

Chusonji Temple

Chusonji Temple was founded by Fujiwara Kiyohira (the first generation of the Fujiwara Clan. The clan had wielded enough strength before Minamoto-no Yoritomo ruled this district).

The temple has the magnificent and brilliant characteristic of Heian Culture. In 1189, when the Tohoku district was conquered by Yoritomo, Chusonji Temple was burnt down, but Konjiki-doh (Golden Hall) and other cultural properties which escaped the fire well present before us the splendor of the original temple.

Near this temple there is a garden attached to Motsuji Temple which was founded by Fujiwara Motohira (the second in descent).

Sendai and Matsushima

The coast of Sendai Bay, which is embraced by Ojika Peninsula, is further indented in the middle and forms a small bay. On the small islands in the bay, more than 200 in all, pine trees grow thick, reflecting themselves upon the ultra-marine blue of the sea. Here is Matsushima ('Pine Islands'), one of Japan's "Scenic Trio*". You can enjoy a beautiful view of Matsushima from the Special Viewing House and Godai Hall built on the seashore. There is also the famous Zuiganji Temple.

Sendai is reached in three hours from Tokyo, and Matsushima is 20 minutes from Sendai by train. There is also airplane service from Haneda, Tokyo.

* Other two are Ama-no-hashidate in Kyoto Pref., and Miyajima in Hiroshima Pref.

Rikuchu Kaigan National Park

This is the indented part of the Pacific coast covering the distance of 930 miles. Forming a part of the Kitakami Mountains, this coast has long been eroded by the violent waves. There are many deeply indented reefs and rocks in and near Jodogahama Beach at Miyako.

There are two great stalactite grottoes, Ryusen-do Cave and Akka-do Cave to the north-west of Miyako. The Akka-do recently discovered has not been fully investigated yet, but the length of the cave is said to surpass that of a cave at Akiyoshidai in Yamaguchi Pref., which had been considered the largest in Japan.

29

Oga Peninsula

The peninsula, situated to the north-west of Akita Pref., juts out into the Sea of Japan. It was once an island, but became connected with the Main Island by the banks of drift sand. And that part of the sea-water which the sand banks enclosed inside the peninsula was the Hachirogata Lagoon, a major portion of which has been converted into farm land by a gigantic reclamation project. The upper reaches of the Omono River form the Yokote Basin. The Yokote Basin is noted for its Bonden Festival (Feb. 17th) and *Kamakura* and the Tanabata Festival of Yuzawa City.

Among others, the Kanto Festival at Akita (Aug. 5 to 7) and Nishimonai Bon Folk Dance at Ugo in the same prefecture are festivals of rich local color.

They say plenty of pretty women are in and near Akita. The women in *smock-frock* in the Shonai, the Akita and Noshiro plains, are so attractive that they seem to be the choice of Japanese customs and manners.

Bandai-Asahi National Park

Mt. Bandai, Goshiki Numa, and Lake Inawashiro

Lake Inawashiro is about four hours by train from Ueno. It is situated at the foot of Mt. Bandai, around which are numerous lakes and ponds. Especially beautiful are a group of small lakes called Goshiki Numa ('The Lakes of Various Colors'), whose water presents various marvellous colors because of the sphagnum and metal ions contained in it. Aizuwakamatsu City, situated near here, is noted for its lacquerware.

Dewa Sanzan (The Three Mountains of Dewa)

These mountains are known as the seat of *Shugen-do,* a kind of Buddhist asceticism based on the combination of mountain worship and Buddhism. The three mountains are Mt. Gassan, Mt. Haguro and Mt. Yudono. On Mt. Haguro there are 2,500 stone steps and a temple with a thatched roof stands among the Japanese cedar trees there. There is bus service from Tsuruoka Station on the Uetsu Line.

Snow covered trees, at Mt. Zao.

A graceful part of Rikuchu Fiord.

Basho

Haiku and *Oku-no Hosomichi* (*The Narrow Road of Oku*)

Haiku is an extremely short form of poetry peculiar to Japan. It originated from an older form of poetry called *Waka,* and flourished in the Edo period (1600–1867) chiefly among samurai and *chonin* (tradesmen). Basho is one of the most highly evaluated *haiku* poets of the Edo period, being rivaled only by Buson.

While Buson took a comparatively affirmative attitude toward nature and wrote *haiku* with a heartfelt sympathy for all living things, Basho laid the basis of his philosophy upon Buddhism and showed a strict observation of life, linking nature with man in the essential. *Oku-no Hosomichi* is the most widely known of his works. It consists of *haiku* poems and travel accounts which he wrote while, setting out from Edo (now Tokyo), he travelled in the Tohoku and the Hokuriku districts. The philosophy of this poet, who was a traveller half his lifetime, will be read in the opening sentences of *Oku-no Hosomichi:*

> The months and days are the travellers of eternity. The years that come and go are also voyagers. Those who float away their lives on boats or who grow old leading horses are forever journeying, and their home is wherever their travels take them. Many of the men of old died on the road, and I too for years past have been stirred by the sight of a solitary cloud drifting with the wind to ceaseless thoughts of roaming. . . . .   (Translated by Donald Keene)

When he went down to Osaka, he fell ill, and died in 1694 at the age of 51, after completing the following poem:

> *Tabi ni yande   yume wa kareno wo kake meguru.*
> (Ill on a journey, I wander in my endless dreams on the withered moorland still.)

Yomeimon Gate of Toshogu Shrine, a feature of Nikko.

The Kanto district consists of Tokyo Metropolis and six prefectures. It needs considerable space to explain the industries, cultural features, and sights of the Tokyo and Tokyo—Hakone districts, so this book has provided separate chapters on the two districts.

The most important role the Kanto district plays in supporting the Tokyo-Yokohama and the Tokyo-Chiba Industrial zones is to supply them with water and electric power.

In the Kanto plain, the Tone River, which has the largest drainage area in Japan (3,169 acres), is an important source of water for agriculture, service water, and water-power generation.

Nikko

Nikko is now an internationally known sightseeing spot in Japan. The central feature is the Nikko Toshogu Shrine. It was built in 1636 by Tokugawa Hidetada and Iemitsu to be dedicated to Tokugawa Ieyasu.

A shrine is a building for Shintoist worship, Shinto meaning "Way of Gods". The building served not only the purpose of enshrining the gods, but also the purpose of filling the visitors in religious awe by showing the greatness of a god or man of great deeds. The Toshogu Shrine is no exception. It was completed by a group of master architects, engravers and craftsmen of the time, who competed with one another in skill to make it more elaborate, more gorgeous, and more graceful.

Following the approach for a while through the huge Japanese cedar trees over one thousand years old, you will see the five-storied pagoda and the lanterns. In the Toshogu Shrine there are 121 lanterns in all—102 stone lanterns, 17 bronze, and 2 iron ones.

Of all the buildings probably the most attractive is the Yomeimon Gate. The Gate has another name meaning "a gate so wonderful that one tarries all day long admiring its beauty". Shining with magnificence and splendor, it symbolizes the Toshogu Shrine.

At the back of the Yomeimon Gate is the main sanctuary. The Karamon Gate is the door to the sanctuary, and is no less attractive than Yomeimon. Of special interest are the ascending and descending dragons and the figures of the ancient Chinese sages carved on the pillars and gables.

The Festival of Nikko is held on May 18. It is famous for its procession of people in samurai armor.

Besides the cultural assets mentioned above, Nikko boasts a beautiful landscape and hot springs. At the foot of Mt. Nantai lies Lake Chuzenji, which may be reached by cable-car from Nikko. Lake Chuzenji was formed when the Daiya River was dammed by the lava from the eruption of Mt. Nantai. The great Kegon Waterfall is just the outlet of the lake, measuring 320 feet in height. Between Lake Chuzenji and the Spa of Yumoto is the pastoral Senjo-ga-hara plain, where beautiful streams are trickling down the rocks.

Near the lake there are the spas of Yumoto and Kotoku, and to the north of Nikko Station are the Kinugawa and Kawaji hot-springs.

KANTO

The huge arch dam of Yagisawa, Gumma Pref.

Mt. Asama

This mountain, forming the boundary between Nagano Prefecture and Gumma Prefecture, ranks beside Mt. Aso as one of the most famous active volcanoes in Japan. *Oni-oshidashi Iwa* (literally 'rocks pushed out by *Oni,* a monster'), which was formed by lava from Mt. Asama, tells of dreadful forces of nature. Karuizawa, not far from the mountain, is a summer resort.

Hot Springs

Hot water is gushing out almost everywhere in the mountain areas around the Kanto plain, bordered as it is by the Nasu-Asama volcanic range. Those areas combine to form one of the most famous hot-spring resorts in the country. Among others, Isobe, Ikaho, Minakami, Shirane, Kinugawa, Shiobara, and Nasu are the noted hot-spring resorts that are visited by the relaxation-seekers not only from the neighboring prefectures but also from Nagano, Niigata, and the Tohoku district. Blessed with fresh streams, these hot-spring resorts look marvellous in the season of crimson leaves.

Mito City

Mito City is the castle town of the Mito Clan of which the second generation is Mito Mitsukuni, a grand-son of Ieyasu, the founder of the Tokugawa Shogunate Government. Mitsukuni was such an outstanding figure that he directly helped the Tokugawa Shogunate as a vice-generalissimo. The most famous in Mito City are the plum trees of Kairakuen Garden. In the past plum flowers were more favored than cherry-blossoms as the flowers that bloom to tell the coming of spring. The plum blossoms are at their best in February and March.

Hitachi's seaside factories, Hitachi City in Ibaraki Pref.

Suigo (The Country of Water)

Suigo is the name of an area in Ibaraki Pref. where the Tone River borders on Lake Kasumi-ga-ura. Particularly beautiful are a network of watercourses and the rural landscape. You enjoy the landscape on a boat handled by a girl in an antique-style *smock-frock* and the sight of numerous flowers blooming on the shore. Not far from there are two shrines, Kashima Shrine (in Ibaraki) and Katori Shrine (in Chiba). The festivals of the two shrines are known all over Japan.

Lake Kasumi-ga-ura (110 sq. mi.) is the largest in Japan next to Lake Biwa.

A new port was constructed in the near-by Kashima Straits. It turns out a port capable of letting in huge 100,000 ton-class ships, and has now the focus of the world's attention as an epoch-making development.

Narita-san Temple

This temple, situated across the Tone to the south of Lake Kasumi-ga-ura, is a famous temple of esoteric Buddhism (*Mikkyo*). It is said that if a car driver possesses an amulet bought at this temple, he can escape traffic accidents. Drivers all over Japan never forget to visit the temple.

New Tokyo International Airport

On May 20, 1978, New Tokyo International Airport opened in Narita which is at a distance of about 66 km from Tokyo. Covering the total available area of 1,065 hectares (of which 550 hectares are actually in use as of 1983), about 180 airplanes depart and arrive every day, with about 24,000 passengers a day. Between April 1982 and March 1983, the new airport saw a total of 8,766,484 passengers getting on and off.

Between Narita and Tokyo, Keisei Skyliner, JNR and special bus services are available.

Suigo province.

New Tokyo International Airport.

TOKYO

A general view of
Akasaka-Mitsuke
and its vicinity.

The population of Tokyo is 11,670,264 the number of registered automobiles 2,793,289 and 180 airplanes leave and arrive at Tokyo International Airport daily. But these numbers are not so important as is the fact that they are constantly changing. The population of Tokyo, for instance, was only 8,000,000 twenty years ago.

Tokyo is situated almost in the middle of the arc-forming Islands of Japan, is 50 miles from east to west in width, and 13 miles from north to south. Three-fourths of the city feature those kinds of rural landscape which will be found in any part of Japan.

However, as it is expected to develop further in the immediate future, the city may be reasonably called "Tokyo Metropolis," including a group of neighboring cities on the coast of Tokyo Bay. "There is no true sky above Tokyo," wrote a certain Japanese poet. The sky above Tokyo has offen been clouded by the waste gas of motorcars and the heavy smoke from factory chimneys. It is said that one hundred years ago Mt. Fuji, 100 miles away, could be clearly seen from Tokyo.

Tokyo International Airport is situated in Chiba Prefecture, Tokyo. Opened in 1978, it now covers 550 hectare in area. From here to the center of the metropolis various transportation services are available for the convenience of passengers. Highways have been remarkably improved since 1964, the year when the Olympic Games were held in Tokyo. The nine express highways (Route Nos. 1 to 9) connect the heart of the metropolis and such 'sub-hearts' as Shinjuku and Shibuya. But the increase of automobiles, in spite of such rapid improvement of the roads, has brought about increasing traffic congestion in every part of the city. According to the statistics, the number of traffic accidents which occurred in 1982 was 85 daily. Every broadcasting station in Tokyo is constantly reporting the traffic conditions of the main areas of the city, to give warning to the car drivers.

Elevated electric railways surround the heart of Tokyo. They are called Yamanote-Sen (Yamanote Belt Line), and are Tokyo's arteries. Inside this Belt Line are situated the National Diet Building, government offices, foreign embassies (which number 118 in all, as of October, 1982), colleges and universities, libraries, and other important buildings. The eastern parts outside the Yamanote Line, popularly called *shitamachi* (downtown sections), were once places where common people lived, whereas the western parts are mostly the residential districts of people who work in Marunouchi and other central business quarters. Private electric railroads connect these western areas and the principal stations of the Yamanote Line, which are crowded every morning and evening with the total number of commuters, 14,000,000 including workers and students. The subway routes in Tokyo are being rapidly expanded to increase the transportation capacity in the city, which is said to have reached its limit.

Most of the commuters flow into the Metropolis from the adjoining cities and prefectures. Around Tokyo new towns or so-called "bed-towns" are appearing one after another, where there are numerous rows of residential buildings popularly called "danchi" (apartment blocks on a large scale).

Here, something must be said about the bullet train Japan is boasting of. It surprised the whole world when it ran on the Tokaido Shinkansen Line at the speed of 124 miles an hour. Today it can cover the distance of 736 miles between Tokyo and Hakata (Fukuoka Pref.) in less than 7 hours. The comfortable cars with rows of five seats abreast, are shut out from the outside and receive little oscillation and noise. Sight-seeing tourists to the west can save a lot of time by using the Shinkansen Line, or airplanes. The bullet trains run about 80 times a day between Tokyo and Osaka, and they are used by 80,000 to 100,000 people on week days, and by 100,000 to 150,000 on holidays.

About 344,000 passengers a day utilize Tokyo — Hakata line.

The Important Places of Tokyo

It would take at least a month to visit all the important places of Tokyo one by one. But, if you use a special sight-seeing bus (Hato Bus), you will be able to see the general sights of Tokyo in a short time. However, in order to look into Tokyo as it really is, you will find it necessary to use your legs and visit the places assiduously one by one.

The Imperial Palace

The map of Tokyo is more easily read by starting from the Imperial Palace. This Palace is the residence and office of the Emperor. It is situated on a spacious green belt covering 260 acres, and surrounded by moats on all sides. The great stone wall presents a majestic view, reminding us of the old Edo Castle.

Imperial Palace in the snow.

The Tokyo Tower

Completed in 1958, the Tower is 1,043 feet above sea-level, slightly higher than the Effel Tower of Paris. Like the Empire State Building in New York City, it can be seen from any part of Tokyo. It is a tower built for transmitting radio waves, and is used by 6 television and 58 radio stations. The tower looks beautiful at night, with all its lights on from top to bottom. To have constructed such a tall structure in a country of frequent typhoons and earthquakes is a credit to the superiority of Japanese architecture and building materials.

The Palace Plaza
(The Outer Garden of the Imperial Palace)

This plaza, which lies between the two moats surrounding the Palace, is probably one of the largest and most beautiful in the world. It is said that in the Edo period there were some 300 houses built on this plaza for the daimios coming up from all over Japan. The *daimio* was a Japanese feudal lord. The Tokugawa Bakufu ordered the daimios in local provinces to come up to Edo in order to put them under its direction, and their wives and children were compelled to live in these houses. Today, this plaza has become an attractive public square with a beautiful green lawn where people enjoy strolling. A large fountain stands there, too, in commemoration of the present Crown Prince's marriage, which took ·place in 1959.

Marunouchi

The area between the Imperial Palace and Tokyo Station is called Marunouchi. With many tall buildings, important banks, firms, and the Central Post Office, Marunouchi forms one great office town. With numerous business facilities, Marunouchi symbolizes the gigantic activities and energy of the Japanese economy.

The National Diet Building

The areas which lie south of the Imperial Palace are called Nagatacho and Kasumigaseki, which teem with many central organs of the Japanese government. The Diet Building is a unique structure which was constructed in 1936, all with domestic materials. With a tower 200 feet high in the middle, it has the assembly rooms of the two Houses in both wings. Seen dirctly from above, it is shaped like the Chinese character 日 , the abbreviation of Japan, 日本 in Japanese.

North of the Diet Building are seen the buildings of the Ministries of Education, Science and Culture, Health and Welfare, International Trade and Industry, Agriculture, Forestry and Fishery, Construction, and Justice, and the Supreme Court and the Metropolitan Police Office.

And to the east lies Hibiya Park, and further in the east is a section of theatres and road-show movie houses, including the Imperial Theatre and the Nissei Theatre.

RAILWAYS
IN TOKYO

JNR = Japanese
National Railways

The National Stadium of Kasumigaoka

About a mile west of the Palace, is another spacious park. It is the Outer Garden of Meiji Shrine, in one section of which stands the National Stadium of Kasumigaoka, which has a seating capacity for 75,000 people.

The Stadium was built at the time of the Asian Games, and some 100,000 people assembled there at the opening ceremony of the Tokyo Olympics.

A mile further to the west of the Stadium stands the National Gymnasium of Yoyogi. This is where the swimming contests were held in the Tokyo Olympics. The gymnasium has a hanging roof which is shaped like a shell turned upside down. It was constructed upon a design prepared by Prof. Kenzo Tange of the University of Tokyo. The floor is 6 acres in area, with seats for 12,000 persons. The swimming pools are turned into a skating rink in winter.

The National Stadium.

Native style gardens in Shinjuku Gyoen Park.

The Shinjuku Gardens

Together with Hibiya Park, these are typical Western style gardens. Because the planner was a Frenchman, it is said that the rows of plane trees in the Gardens look like the woods of Boulogne and Versailles.

Meiji Shrine

The word Meiji was used as a name for the 45 years from 1868 to 1912, and the emperor during these years was called Emperor Meiji. The Meiji Shrine was erected in 1920 to be dedicated to this great Emperor and his consort. The present building is a replica of the original shrine which was burnt down in the War. The precinct occupies an area of 170 acres. Five-sixths, that is, 126,000, of the many trees growing there were donated from all over the country.

The Outer Garden of Meiji Shrine

The Outer Garden commemorates the great funeral of the Emperor Meiji, which took place in 1912. It was constructed over a period of 10 years from 1917 to 1927. The construction was made possible largely by the donations from the people of Japan.

Besides the National Stadium mentioned above, here are the Meiji Memorial Picture Gallery, the Meiji Shrine Baseball Stadium, Chichibunomiya Rugby Field, and the Meiji Shrine Swimming Pool.

Yasukuni Shrine

Founded in 1869, the Shrine is dedicated to the souls of 2,400,000 brave men killed on the battlefields, including the girl students (known as *Himeyuri* or Red Starlilies) who were killed in Okinawa during the Pacific War. The great *torii* or arch, seventy feet high, is the largest one in bronze in Japan. The *torii* is the symbol of the sanctuary, but its origin is not known.

Incidentally, there is the Tomb of the Unknown Soldier of World War II to the west of the Palace. Even today you can never visit the tomb without finding some flowers placed before the charnel-house.

Between the Shrine and the Imperial Palace is a quiet section of parks. A conspicuous octagonal building in this area is Budokan Hall, which was built for the Judo matches of the 1964 Olympics. It was also here that the Beetles were received by young people with wild enthusiasm.

Let us next visit the northern areas just outside the Belt Line.

The Ginza

The Ginza is beautiful at night. The neon signs, our man-made flowers, color the night sky. Travellers from abroad often admire the variety of colors and the innumerable neon signs in Tokyo.

The area called Ginza is a comparatively small space between the Imperial Palace and Tokyo Bay, divided into two by a street about a mile long from north to south. In the Edo period silver coins, then current, were minted there; hence the name Ginza or Silver Guild. Today, however, the Ginza is a place at which many coins are spent. Many noted shops, all long-established, such as Mikimoto for pearls, and Shiseido for cosmetics, attract passers-by with their beautifully decorated windows. There is also an increasing number of department stores. The Ginza is lastly a place of many restaurants and bars boasting of their top-class atmospheres.

Besides the Ginza, there are in Tokyo many other bustling quarters, such as Shinjuku, Shibuya, and Ikebukuro. Tokyo is thus a city of widely scattered consumers.

Asakusa

If Ginza is a town for 'upperclass' people, then Asakusa is a town exclusively for 'common' people. This is understood by the fact that the center of the town is Sensoji Temple, one of the oldest in Tokyo. The religious beliefs of the common people remain deeply implanted in their customs, and will never be destroyed by any calamity. Asakusa retains vivid traces of the Edo times. The present Kan-non-doh or Sensoji Temple (60 feet in height), completed on 1975, is a faithful reconstruction of the old. The principal image (Honzon) is that of Kan-non,the Deity of Mercy, handed down from the 7th century, and cannot be seen elsewhere.

The vicinity of Sensoji Temple is crowded with numerous souvenir-shops, eating houses, saloons and bars, and theaters. The yearly festival of Asakusa is one of the liveliest in Tokyo.

If you walk around in Asakusa and Ginza, you will be able to see nearly all classes of people. And because most of their faces reveal no names in particular, you can see in them the faces of the Japanese as they really are.

53

Ginza 4-chome junction (above) and Ginza street.

Sensoji Temple of Asakusa. Worshippers burn incense rods to ward off evil before going up to the main altar.

Many souvenir shops stand side by side along *Nakamise* Alley on the way to the Sensoji.

A bird-view of Tokyo. Tokyo Station of National Railway is seen above. The Marunouchi office town lies in front of Tokyo Station.

MORE OF TOKYO

Such brief information as given above cannot cover all of Tokyo. In the following pages, therefore, you will find further explanations about Tokyo—its minor but no less important constituents.

Let us see the people working busily. Let us have a look at the troubles and contradictions the world's largest city is involved in. It is because Tokyo's vitality and weaknesses are nothing less than the vitality and weaknesses of entire Japan. And in this big city anything can happen, but you will come to know that it is nothing surprising to most Japanese, however strange it may look to a foreign eye.

Line-up of a Kabuki drama, *The Dammari*.

The Kabuki Theater.

Kabuki Theater

This is a theater for staging the traditional Japanese play, Kabuki, but is often used today by popular singers for one-man shows. The building looks old-fashioned, but has been frequently reconstructed since it was founded in 1889. It is reached very shortly from the eastern side of the Ginza.

Other large theaters in Tokyo include the National Theater, Imperial Theater and Nissei Theater. There are also the Toho Theater, which stages an all-girl operetta, and the Meijiza and Shinjuku Koma Theater.

Tokyo Monorail

There is an electric train that bestrides a single concrete railway to cover the distance of eight miles from Haneda Airport to the central parts of the Metropolis. This electric train began service in 1964, and is doubtless one of the world's rarest examples that commercially pay.

Since the elevated rail is built along Tokyo Bay, it commands a wonderful view.

The Age of Skyscrapers

In 1963 an amendment to the building law made it generally possible to build a structure exceeding 100 feet in height, which the law previously had forbidden to avoid greater earthquake damages. After this, many skyscrapers began to appear, some reaching 700 or 800 feet in height from the ground. The tallest of those is a 750-foot-height building which was erected near the Shinjuku Central Park.

Nobody would be surprised if this took place in solid-ground Manhattan Island, but it sure is an amazing thing for a country like Japan. Indeed, it is only through the advancement of Japanese architectural research and the production of strong light materials that such tall buildings have come to be erected on her unstable ground. Older buildings, which are all less than 100 feet in height and bulky in size, leave less space between them. (Japan is not a 'spacious' country.) With the appearance of skyscrapers, it will be possible to have this kind of narrow 'valley' between the buildings enlarged into public squares.

Increasing skyscrapers in Shinjuku Sub-Metropolis.

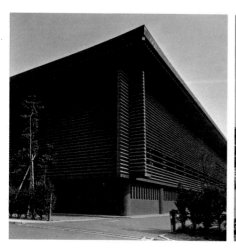

(Far left) The exterior of the National Theater is originated from the old *godown* style called *azekura-zukuri* typical to that seen at Shosoin, Todaiji Temple of Nara.
(Left) Budokan Hall, the center of Japanese traditional sports.
(Below left) The Komazawa Physical Olympic Park, in western suburbs of Tokyo, was constructed for the 1964 Olympics with many unique designs—press gondolas of main stadium like huge nails, the symbolic tower modeled after temple pagodas, the pentagonal gymnasium, etc.
(Below) Tokyo St. Mary Cathedral.

The monorail runs over the Tokyo Bay in parallel with Route No.1 highway (above).
CD Production Line, Sony Audio Inc.

Tokyo St. Mary Cathedral

Besides the old shrines and temples, seats of the religious recently brought into Japan are seen here and there in Tokyo. These churches are quite unique in outward form, and among them, St. Mary Cathedral, which was designed in 1964 by Japan's leading architect, Kenzo Tange, looks super-modern. With its exterior made entirely of stainless-steel, the Cathedral houses Japan's largest pipe-organ.

The dome of a Moslem church in Shibuya is truly Saracenic, while Tsukiji Honganji, an old Buddhist temple, reveals an ancient Indian style. Nicolai Cathedral in Kanda, built in 1871, is Byzantinesque and adds a unique figure to the scenery of Tokyo.

Sony

Today the name of Sony as well as Mt. Fuji is known all over the world as symbolizing Japan, especially Japan's industry. In talking about this company, which has come to be known worldwide in a short space of time since its foundation in 1946, it is necessary to regard it as a typical example of the rapidly advanced enterprises in postwar Japan, as well as boasting of the superiority of its transistor radios and TV sets. And you may remember that what supports Sony is more the scientific way of its management (surpassing even that of greater enterprises), than the apparent superiority of its engineering.

The show-room of Sony is in Ginza. It is a unique building where visitors are first carried by the elevator as high as the roof and then go slowly down to see the exhibited articles.

Tokyo Central Wholesale Market

Six blocks from the Ginza is a wholesale market which is popularly called *Uo Ichiba* or fish market. One of the liveliest markets of the world, it manages about 3,000 tons of fish a day, all of which Tokyoites consume in a single day. It is well-furnished and boasts of being always clean.

When foreign leaders in fisheries visit Japan, they never fail to come here, and are always surprised at how bustling it is.

The Press and the Mass-communication Media

Tokyo is also the center of mass media. The Japanese press is an enterprise which has a scale probably unparalleled in the world. The three largest newspapers—the Asahi, the Mainichi, and the Yomiuri—have in all an unbelievable daily circulation of some 20,749,000. The daily page number of the three papers averages 30. One-fifth of 170 papers in Japan (including only those associated with the Japan Newspaper Publishers and Editors Association) are daily published in Tokyo. Three biggest papers have a voice in various fields and are not tied to any particular political party. The newspapers are playing an important role in providing a material background to every cultural undertaking.

Television as well as the press has had great influence upon all the Japanese. Almost all households possess TV sets, and the number of TV sets in Japan exceeds 30,000,000. The number of TV stations (including radio stations) is 12,816 of which 7 channels can be selected in the Tokyo area.

A national network of color-telecasting was completed in March 1965. At present, all programs are color-telecasted.

Publication

Japan is famous for her extensive publication of books, including translations of various foreign books, and various magazines, including weeklies, monthlies, quarterlies and yearbooks of various genre – literature, sports, amusement, gosship, etc.

There are also various English newspapers, including Asahi Evening News, Mainichi Daily News, The Daily Yomiuri, The Japan Times, Shipping & Trade News. "Tour Companion" also contains much useful information for foreign visitors.

A brisk auction of tuna, at the Tokyo Central Market. (Left)

The Head Office of Asahi newspaper, one of the three major newspaper firms in Japan.

Waseda University.

The University of Tokyo

As of 1982, there were 981 colleges and universities in Japan, of which 184 were in Tokyo. No other country except the United States has so many. The number of students, including those from abroad, reaches 2,191,922. Approximately 30 percent of the total number of high school graduates wish to enter college.

Among those universities, the position of Tokyo or Kyoto University in Japan may be compared to that of Oxford and Cambridge in England. Many of those who occupy leading positions in every field have graduated from Tokyo or Kyoto University. Tokyo University was founded in 1877, and Kyoto University in 1897.

Private colleges in Tokyo, numbering the greater part of all the colleges and universities, have each a long history of research in the field of either medicine, science and technology, law, economics, or the like.

The National Museum.

The Yoyogi Gymnasiums.

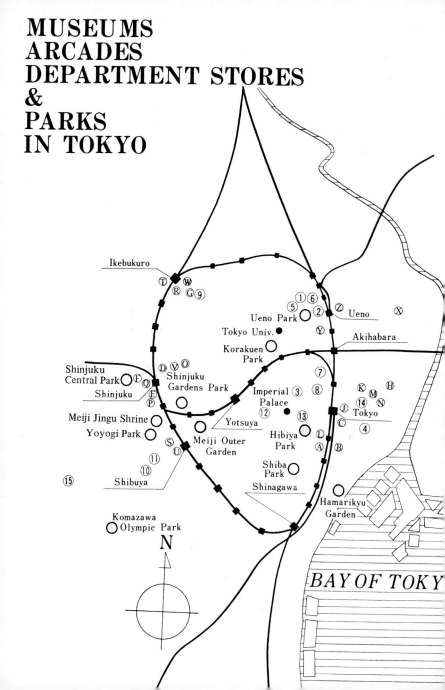

MUSEUMS
ARCADES
DEPARTMENT STORES
&
PARKS
IN TOKYO

Ikebukuro

Ⓣ Ⓦ
Ⓡ Ⓖ ⑨

① ⑥
⑤ ②
Ⓩ Ueno
Ⓧ
Ueno Park
Tokyo Univ. ●
Ⓨ
Akihabara
Korakuen
Park

Shinjuku
Central Park Ⓕ Ⓓ Ⓥ Ⓞ
Ⓠ Shinjuku
Shinjuku Gardens Park
⑦
Ⓟ
Imperial ③ ⑧
Palace Ⓚ Ⓜ Ⓗ
⑭
⑫ Ⓝ
Ⓙ Tokyo
Ⓒ
Meiji Jingu Shrine ●
Yoyogi Park Yotsuya ⑬ ④
Ⓛ
Hibiya Ⓐ Ⓑ
Ⓢ Meiji Outer Park
⑪ Ⓤ Garden
⑩
⑮ Shiba
Shibuya Park
Shinagawa
Hamarikyu
Garden
Komazawa
Olympic Park
N

BAY OF TOKYO

MAIN MUSEUMS IN TOKYO

TOKYO NATIONAL MUSEUM ①
(Ueno Park)
  Historical arts and crafts. The oldest museum in Japan.
NATIONAL MUSEUM OF WESTERN ART ②
(Ueno Park)
  Mainly consisted of Matsukata Collection.
NATIONAL MUSEUM OF MODERN ART ③
(Takebashi, near the Imperial Palace)
  Mecca of world modern art.
BRIDGESTONE GALLERY ④
(Kyobashi, near the Tokyo Station)
  Mr. Ishibashi's Collection of western art.
METROPOLITAN ART GALLERY ⑤
(Ueno Park)
  Many important exhibitions of art groups are held.
NATIONAL SCIENCE MUSEUM ⑥
(Ueno Park)
  Covered all fields of science.
TRANSPORTATION MUSEUM ⑦
(Kanda)
COMMUNICATIONS MUSEUM ⑧
(Otemachi, near the Tokyo Station)
ANCIENT ORIENT MUSEUM ⑨
(in Sunshine City, Higashi-Ikebukuro)
MODERN LITERATURE MUSEUM ⑩
(Komaba, near Tokyo University)
JAPAN FOLKCRAFT MUSEUM ⑪
(Komaba)
SUNTORY GALLERY ⑫
(Suntory Bldg, Akasaka)
IDEMITSU ART GALLERY ⑬
(Palace Bldg, Marunouchi)
YAMATANE MUSEUM OF ART ⑭
(Kayabacho, Nihonbashi)
GOTOH ART MUSEUM ⑮
(Kaminoge, Setagayaku)

SHOPPING ARCADES & TOWNS

International Arcade (near the Imperial Hotel, under the Yamanote elevated railway.) Ⓐ
Sukiyabashi Shopping Center (between Ginza Street and the Yurakucho Station, under the highway No. 4.) Ⓑ
Yaesu Underground Center (near Tokyo Station.) Ⓒ
Shinjuku Subnade (under the east side of Shinjuku Station.) Ⓓ
Keio Mole, Odakyu Ace (under the west side of Shinjuku Station.) Ⓔ
High-rise Building Street in Shinjuku Sub-Metropolis (7 minutes from the west side of Shinjuku Station.) Ⓕ
Sunshine City & Alpa (10 minutes distance from Ikebukuro Station.) Ⓖ
Tokyo City Air Terminal Shop (near Ningyo-cho Station.) Ⓗ
Tokyo Gateway Shop (New Tokyo International Airport Terminal Building, Narita.) Ⓘ

DEPARTMENT STORES

GINZA   (See page 74 - 75)

Hankyu. Matsuya. Matsuzakaya. Mitsukoshi.

NEAR GINZA

Daimaru (Tokyo Station) Ⓙ
Mitsukoshi Main Store (Near the Tokyo Station, called Nihombashi Mitsukoshi.) Ⓚ
Sogo (Very near the Yurakucho Station) Ⓛ
Tokyu (At the Nihombashi junction) Ⓜ
Takashimaya (Near the Tokyo Station) Ⓝ

ALL QUARTERS

Isetan (Shinjuku) Ⓞ
Keio (Very near the Shinjuku Station) Ⓟ
Odakyu (Near the Shinjuku Station) Ⓠ
Seibu (Ikebukuro Terminal Bldg. and Shibuya) Ⓡ Ⓢ
Tobu (Eastern side of Ikebukuro Terminal Bldg.) Ⓣ
Tokyu (Very near the Shibuya Station) Ⓤ
Mitsukoshi, in Shinjuku and Ikebukuro Ⓥ Ⓦ
Matsuya, in Asakusa Ⓧ
Matsuzakaya, in Ueno (Near the Okachimachi Station) Ⓨ
Keisei (Ueno) Ⓩ

- jewel & watch
  ISEI A-3
  SEIKODO A-1
  YAMAZAKI A-8
  TENSHODO B-24
  MIKIMOTO B-18
  NIPPONDO C-11
  MIWA C-53
  NISSHINDO D-6
  KYOBIDO D-12

- shoes & sandals
  HIGUCHI B-3
  YOSHINOYA B-17
  KANEMATSU B-15
  AMERIKAYA B-28 C-13
  WASHINGTON C-14
  DAIANA C-45
  FUTABAYA C-52 C-59
  ST-MARRY D-7

- pouches
  TANIZAWA A-7 C-29
  GINSEIDO A-15
  HAKUBOTAN C-8
  DAI KOKUYA C-12
  TENCHIDO C-48

- camera
  HAMADA SHOKAI A-10
  SUKIYA C-24

  KODAK B-27
  UTSUKI C-34
  ORIENT D-19

- restaurant & parlor
  ASTER A-4
  DAI SHIN A-5
  OLYMPIC A-13
  RANGETSU B-6
  GINZA SAISON B-9
  KIMURAYA B-20
  VAN B-26
  CHIKUYOTEI C-2
  SARASHINA C-3
  SENBIKIYA C-23 D-24
  MIKASAKAIKAN C-25
  KETELS C-26
  SUEHIRO C-39
  DAIMASU C-46
  COZY CORNER C-56
  TEN'ICHI C-58
  HAPPOEN C-62
  BENIHANA C-64
  ASHOKA D-3
  TENKUNI D-20
  SHISEIDO D-21
  ART COFFEE D-30

- confectionery
  FUGETSUDO A-17 C-57
  FUJIYA B-29 C-42

  MORINAGA C-15
  AKEBONO C-17
  TOKYO YOKAN C-49
  TORAYA D-9
  TATSUTANO D-11

- beer pub
  LION C-5 D-1
  NEW TOKYO C-65

- gallery
  SAEGUSA B-5
  TAMAYA B-22
  BUN SHUN C-27
  NICHIDO C-33 D-16
  KIKUCHI C-60
  SHIRAI C-63
  TAMENAGA D-14
  FUJII D-15
  KABUTOYA D-23

- books
  KYOBUNKAN B-16
  JENA'S (KONDO) C-18
  ASAHIYA C-37
  FUKUYA D-22

- stationery
  ITOYA A-14
  BUNSHODO B-8
  KYU KYODO C-10
  KURO SAWA C-41

GINZA

A   B

① ② ③ ④   ⑤   ⑪   ⑫ ⑬ ⑭   ①   ⑨ ⑩ ⑪ ⑫ ⑬   ⑭
                                                         ⑮

—1-chome—   —2-chome—   —3-chome— Subway —4-chome—
                                  Ginza Line

⑥ ⑦ ⑧ ⑨   ⑮ ⑯ ⑰ ⑱   ② ③ ④ ⑤ ⑥ ⑦   ⑯ ⑰ ⑱ ⑲ ⑳ ㉑

⑩   ⑧   ㉒   ㉓

                                                        ㉔
                                                        ㉕
                                            ㉗   ㉖

              ⑲   ㉘

                        ⑳   ㉙

HIGHWAY   ㉛ ㉜

• department store
MEITETSU MELSA A-11
MATSUYA B-1
MITSUKOSHI B-14
WAKO B-21
FOOD CENTER B-31
KOA C-6
LIZA C-7
SAN'AI C-9
MEITETSU NEW MELSA C-16
HANKYU C-36
SUKIYABASHI SHOPPING CENTER C-38
MATSUZAKAYA C-40
KOMATSU STORE C-44

• showroom
GINZA MICOM BASE (personal computer) A-2
NIHONSHU ("SAKE") CENTER C-1
NISSAN C-4
MITSUBISHI (electric appliances) C-9
SONY C-32
TOSHIBA (electric appliances) D-2
TOKYO GAS D-4
TOTO D-10
YANASE D-29

• cosmetics
POLA A-9
KANEBO B-2
SHISEIDO D-13

• hotel
NIKKO D-28
DAI'ICHI D-17
GINZA KOKUSAI D-26
MITSUI URBAN D-27

• clothings
EIKOKUYA A-12 C-51
EMBA A-18
TAMAYA B-7
TAYA B-12
MOTOKI B-13 B-25
VAUGU (hats) C-19
SUZUYA C-22
J & R C-30
ICHI BANKAN C-35
JOSÉPHINE C-54

• dry goods
ECHIGOYA A-16
GINZA SILK B-11
SUZUNOYA C-21
MASUIWAYA C-28 C-55
KISHIYA C-31
MAGGIE C-47
KAWAMURA D-18

• china ware
KOYANAGI A-6
TACHIKICHI C-20
KURODA TO-EN D-8

• eye grasses
MATSUSHIMAYA B-4
IWASAKI C-43

• fine arts and antique objects
IKEDAYA C-50
HATOYA C-61

• musical instrument
YAMANO B-19
YAMAHA D-5

• toy
KINTARO B-10

• theater
NAMIKIZA A-19
GINZA BUNKA I-II B-23
TOEI B-30
MARUNOUCHI PICCADILLY B-32
MARUNOUCHI SHOCHIKU B-32
HAKUHINKAN D-25

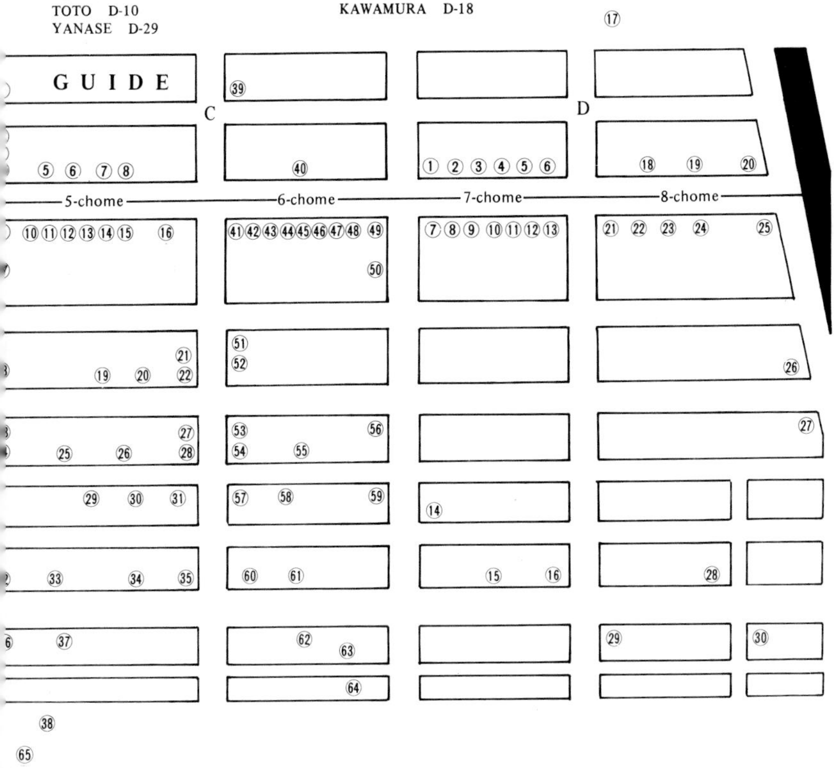
GUIDE
C
D
5-chome
6-chome
7-chome
8-chome
⑰
㊴
⑤ ⑥ ⑦ ⑧
㊵
① ② ③ ④ ⑤ ⑥
⑱ ⑲ ⑳
⑩ ⑪ ⑫ ⑬ ⑭ ⑮ ⑯
㊶ ㊷ ㊸ ㊹ ㊺ ㊻ ㊼ ㊽ ㊾ ㊿
⑦ ⑧ ⑨ ⑩ ⑪ ⑫ ⑬
㉑ ㉒ ㉓ ㉔ ㉕
㉑ ⑲ ⑳ ㉒
(51) (52)
㉖
㉗ ㉕ ㉖ ㉘
(53) (54) (55) (56)
㉗
㉙ ㉚ ㉛
(57) (58) (59)
⑭
㉝ ㉞ ㉟
(60) (61)
⑮ ⑯
㉘
㊲
(62) (63)
㉙ ㉚
(64)
㊳
(65)

The History of Tokyo

About 500 years ago Tokyo was only a poor fishing village. In 1456, at a time of revolts and wars, Ota Dokan built a fortress at the site the Imperial Palace occupies today. Towards the close of the 16th century, Shogun Tokugawa Ieyasu reconstructed it into a great castle. In those days the town in which this castle stood was called "Edo". For the 264 years since then (1603 – 1867), the Tokugawa family held government in Edo and ruled over Japan. This is known as the Edo or Tokugawa period.

The words "Edo" and "Shogun" will often appear in this book. *Shogun* was at first an official title given to any governor of a district, but after Minamoto-no Yoritomo received the title of *shogun* in 1192, it came to designate the ruler of Japan.

In 1869 the imperial house moved to Edo, and Edo was renamed Tokyo, the Eastern Capital of Japan. The next 50 years that Emperor Meiji directly took the helm of state affairs were a chaotic but vigorous age when Japan was making strenuous efforts to assimilate Western civilizations, especially those of Germany, England, America, and France. Since then, the development of Tokyo has been the development of the whole country.

Tokyo has frequently been exposed to complete destruction. In 1854 and 1923 Tokyo was visited by violent earthquakes followed by great fires. The disasters in 1923 destroyed Tokyo almost completely, with 400,000 houses burnt down and more than 100,000 people left dead or missing. In the Pacific War Tokyo was more severely damaged by air-raids.

The present gigantic Tokyo looks like a phoenix risen from its ashes. Nowhere in the great city can you see today traces of the severe wounds. Yet those wounds remain unhealed in the minds of the people.

NATIONAL HOLIDAYS

New Year's Day	January 1st
Adulthood Day	January 15th
Foundation Day	February 11th
Vernal Equinox Day	around March 21st
Emperor's Birthday	April 29th
Constitution Memorial Day	May 3rd
Children's Day	May 5th
Respect-for-age Day	September 15th
Autumnal Equinox Day	around September 23rd
Physical Culture Day	October 10th
Culture Day	November 3rd
Labor Day	November 23rd

CUSTOMS AND MANNERS

Japan has a long history of Shintoism and Buddhism. In Japan the wedding is generally performed according to the Shinto rites, and the funeral according to the Buddhist. Needless to say, the propagation of Christianity is not restricted, so there are many people who celebrate their weddings at Christian churches, but the people who get married at Shinto shrines far outnumber those who do so by either the Buddhist or Christian rites.

In their finest dresses, hundreds of people visit Asakusa Kan-non (Sensoji Temple) in the beginning of the year, and buy *daruma* dolls. There is a custom that those who have the doll supply the eye-pupils to it when they have attained their goals.

Shogatsu (New Year's Day)

The greatest event of the year in Japan like Christmas in Christian countries. We always look forward to New Year's Day, for it is, above all, the time of exchanging New Year cards with our friends and relatives.

On January 1, at the stroke of 12 midnight, all the temples all over the country begin to strike their bells, repeating 108 times to pray for everlasting peace. Then, both young and old put on their finest clothes and visit the shrines. We go to make a New Year's call on our friends and acquaintances, and males drink *sake* with one another. Girls enjoy playing battledore and shuttlecock (*hanetsuki*), boys play top spinning or fly kites, while indoors they play cards with their families and friends.

Formerly *shogatsu* meant the first month of the year from January 1 to 31, but nowadays it is brought to a close on January 7, when the New Year's pine decorations are removed from the gate.

Setsubun

This is the ceremony performed on the eve of the springtide. *Setsubun* was born from an old belief that the gods visit every house and bring it good luck. On the night of *Setsubun* we throw parched beans both inside and outside the house, crying *"Fuku wa uchi! Oni wa soto!"* ("In with luck! Out with devils!"). It is said that in this way we can drive out sickness and evil spirits and enjoy good luck.

Hina Matsuri (The Children's Festival)

A festival for girls is held on March 3, properly called *Hina Matsuri* or *Momo-no Sekku,* which literally means 'Feast of Peach-Blossoms'. On the altars arranged in tiers and covered with a red cloth, we place in order the tiny figures of the Emperor and Empress, samurai, retainers, put peach-blossoms in the room and eat festival dishes.

May 5, the day for boys, called *Tango-no Sekku* is appointed a National Holiday as "Children's Day". On that day we put up cloth carps and adorn the room with warrior dolls.

Children throwing beans in a temple (above).
A department store counter in Osaka. This set of *hina* dolls is worth about 400 dollars (below).

Obon, or Urabon-e

Obon is the name of the Buddhist rites performed generally from July 14 to 16 for the consolation of the deceased families. Every home prepares an altar and burns incense, praying that their souls may ever be peaceful in the next world.

Bon odori (Bon Festival Dance) is one of the programs during the Obon period. (See the section on Bon Odori p. 147.)

Summer Festivals

In Japan, which is under rapid modernization, it is only in the popular festivals and Buddhist events that you can discover the ancient Japan. The shrine festivals are held in spring, summer and autumn, but the most pompous and colorful are in summer. Festivals all over the country show different local colors, but generally people pull the decorated floats or carry portable shrines through the streets, in a tumultuous fashion.

Shichi-Go-San (7-5-3)
(Gala Day for Children aged 7, 5 and 3)

The festival held on Nov. 15 to pray for the children's healthy growth. The parents who have 7-year-old girls, 5-year-old boys, or 3-year-old girls, dress them up and take them to a shrine. The exact origin is not known, but it is said that the festival has the purpose of socially celebrating the children of those ages, for they come to have more power of resistance to disease and so may be regarded as individuals.

The Funeral

Except in the case of ardent Christians, the funeral is performed according to the Buddhist rites. The funeral in Japan, as in other countries, is a scene of bitter grief, and the burial service is even similar to that in Christian countries. The departed is given a Buddhist name, for he is believed to be reborn in another world, and the name is engraved on the tombstone with the date of his death.

The famous cemetries in Tokyo are those at Yanaka, Aoyama and the Tama hills.

81

Cloth carp streaming in the sky in May (above).
Young lads carry about a *mikoshi,* sacred miniature shrine, at the summer festival in Asakusa (below).

An old woman attends
worship with her grand-
children. At Temman-
gu Shrine, Osaka, Nov-
ember 15th (above).
The cemetery of Tama,
Tokyo (below).

TOKYO TO HAKONE

Yokohama is 30 minutes by train from Tokyo. It is 19 miles from Shimbashi, at which the Tokyo-Yokohama streets start. Three highways connect Tokyo and Yokohama. The Tokyo-Yokohama area is Japan's most important industrial factory district, and especially in Kawasaki City, situated at the mouth of the Tama River, numbers of large and small factories stand close together. Occupied with steam-power plants, oil refineries, iron foundries, cement plants, dockyards, and other heavy chemical plants, the area presents a spectacle of Japan's beating heart. You cannot find a single trace of war damage there.

Yokohama

Yokohama ranks with Kobe as one of the busiest and largest seaports in Japan. The long Isolation of Japan in the Edo period ended in 1858 with the opening of Yokohama Harbor. The civilizations of Europe and America flowed into Japan through Yokohama. Today the exports from Yokohama account for 25.8 per cent of Japan's total. It is Japan's third largest city with a population of 2,848,155.

As is often the case with seaports, Yokohama is quite an international town. But in Yokohama, as in Kobe and Nagasaki, all with a long history behind, there is not too much of a merry-making and nasty atmosphere which is usually something inevitable with a new town. Oldtimers in Yokohama are highly critical about 'foreigner worship' seen in many of the younger generation. They still remember earlier pioneers who, though baptized with waves of an advanced culture, were never servile-minded toward the great powers of the world.

There are miles of beautiful landscape along the coast. In Yamashita Park, which commands an entire view of the coast, a lot of people are seen strolling every day.

Lastly, Yokohama Harbor has a mooring capacity of 67 berth.

Enoshima Island

This is a small island located a quarter mile from Katase Beach and is only an hour's bus-ride from Yokohama. In summer the Enoshima-Katase area is crowded with thousands of sea-bathers. A foreign visitor once said that the Japanese naturally like this kind of crowded place, but the truth is that it reveals only one side of the many imbalanced ways that Japan has in itself.

The Shonan Beach, represented by Enoshima, is the most easily accessible bathing resort from Tokyo. Enoshima has the largest yacht harbor in Japan, which was used for the yacht race of the 1964 Tokyo Olympics. In a large pool named "Marine Land," there are several dolphins and whales performing various acrobatic shows. Sometimes they jump up as high as 5 feet above the water, to catch fish thrown by visitors, and sometimes play water polo, quite inimitably.

Kamakura

Though only 15 square miles in area, Kamakura, surrounded by a natural strongfold of hills, was once an important city in Japan. In 1185 Minamoto-no Yoritomo established a government here, to put an end to a period of wars and revolts. This government became the first *Bakufu* or Shogunate Government, which is known as the Kamakura Government. Yoritomo defeated the Taira Clan who had exercised great power in Kyoto, and received the title of *shogun* or 'generalissimo' in 1192. Though power in the government soon passed to other rulers, Kamakura remained the seat of Japanese government until almost 1333.

After the Imperial Court was restored to power, Kamakura made a cultural development as a quiet local city, and because it had many Zen-Buddhist temples, the study of them flourished. Since about 1870 it has become a noted seaside resort, and has also come to be occupied with an increasing number of villas and homes. Kamakura is one hour from Tokyo by train. More than 20,000 people commute every day to Tokyo or Yokohama, for either work or study, and it is said that the number of the people who visit there in four seasons is 20,000,000.

Daibutsu of Kamakura.

Kenchoji Temple, the first of Kamakura Big-Five Temples.

Being an old town, Kamakura has many temples with historical backgrounds. At a small distance from the city area, there stands a huge statue of Budda—*Daibutsu*. This *Daibutsu* cannot rival in size its more famous counterpart at Nara, but the face it has of Budda is said to be a lot handsomer. It has a height of 44 feet. The exact history of the Daibutsu is not known, but it is considered to have been cast about the middle of the 13th century. The temple which concealed the Daibutsu has long since broken down, and today this Daibutsu stands exposed to the sun and wind and is often photographed naked by the visitors.

Atami

Atami is 63 miles from Tokyo and 3 stops from Tokyo Station on the Shinkansen Line. The city is situated at the neck of the Izu Peninsula looking over Sagami Bay. Atami is a popular hot-spring resort, the nearest and most conveniently located from Tokyo, with some 370 hotels and inns operating within the city. Over 7,800,000 gallons of hot water gushes out of the surrounding mountains daily. 'Atami' means 'Hot Sea'. The Hakone Mountains, which shelter Atami in the north, rise gradually from the coast of Sagami Bay, and their sides are terraced with many villas.

Hakone

Just as Atami is a popular seaside hot-spring resort, so Hakone is noted for its mountainside hot-springs. The Hakone Mountains, with a height of only 4,700 feet, have a charm of variety in their figures, and Lake Ashi (known to foreigners as Lake Hakone) adds a great deal to their grandeur. Going up to the mountains is quite easy today. A well-built highway runs between the mountains, and you can enjoy a beautiful view along the highway. Hakone was once a trying place for people travelling on the Tokaido Highway. Even today the highway is frozen over with snow and is often closed for automobiles in mid-winter.

Mt. Fuji as seen from Hakone is also beautiful. And the swift twin-hull boat that carries you from one side of Lake Ashi to the other, and the ropeway overlooking the lake delight the hearts and eyes of the tourists.

A view of Lake Ashi, or Lake Hakone, from the ropeway.

The Shinkansen bullet trains.

Mt. Fuji

A certain professional guide once said:

"You people will be quite disappointed if you stay in Japan and can't see Mt. Fuji on account of bad weather, but it is the same with us. In fact, we feel as if we had done something wrong to you if you can't see it."

Mt. Fuji is the highest mountain (12,388 feet above sea level) in Japan, and rises nearly in the middle of the country. It has a balanced figure of a conical volcano, with a gentle slope starting from as low as the sea level. It stands out conspicuously among the neighboring mountains which are only about 3,000 feet high, and when the sky is clear you can see it even from the sea 100 miles away.

The reason why it is often regarded as a symbol of Japan is that, it not only has geographical charms, but also has been an object of popular religious beliefs since long ago. People replaced the pronounciation of the word 富士, the name of this mountain, by the word 不死 ('immortal') or 不二 ('unparalleled'), both of which are pronounced exactly the same as fu-ji, and thus worshipped the mountain as the dwelling-place of a Natural Deity. This worship was most prevalent during the times when Edo was the center of Japanese government and more and more people came to live there. Mt. Fuji is only 100 miles from Edo (Tokyo). Concealed below the breast in a thick mist peculiar to Japan and with its summit appearing to be floating in mid-air, Mt. Fuji is itself a fantasied, mystic existence. It is quite natural that a shrine should have been erected on the summit and that people should have wished to visit it even once in their lives to feel the spirit of the Deity.

People have come to think this kind of worship groundless, but even today Mt. Fuji is often treated in literature and painting.

If yours is a busy tour, you can see the mountain and its grandeur from the New Tokaido Line, and if you have time to go as far as Hakone, you'll be able to see it better at a closer district.

Mt. Fuji putting on a cloud hat.

"Fuji Behind the Waves" by Katsushika Hokusai. One of the "Thirty-six scenes of Mt.
Fuji." Hokusai (1760–1849) founded and
completed Japanese landscape pictures in
wood-engraving.

GEOGRAPHY

Japan consists of four large islands, Hokkaido, Honshu or Main Island, Shikoku, Kyushu, and more than 3,000 tiny islands. The distance between Japan and the Asian Continent is at the closest 120 miles beyond the Tsushima Islands, which was the commercial gate to Korea and China in ancient times.

Japan has an area of 142,728 square miles, of which only 14.4 per cent is agricultural, the rest being almost entirely mountainous. As the highlands are close to the sea, the currents of rivers are quite rapid. Japan belongs to the temperate zone, the four seasons it has are sharply defined. The four seasons are, by the way, the important natural influences upon her culture.

There are warm and cold currents flowing around the islands of Japan. The warm current is known as *Kuroshio* (Black or Japan Current). It is warm and contains much salt. It flows at an average speed of 2 to 3 knots, the highest being 4 to 5 knots. Coming up from the east of Formosa, it flows toward north-east, a large body of water 6.2 miles wide, along the southern shores of Japan.

The cold current is known as the *Oyashio* or Chishima Current. It flows down from the Arctic regions. It has little salt, and is rich in plankton and other nutritious foods for fishes.

The two currents encounter off the coast of the Tohoku district, creating the largest inshore fishing zone in Japan.

Geology

The islands of Japan have the geological features of both the new and old geological ages. They are formed of groups of comparatively recent mountain ranges, rising and falling, of which Kyushu, Honshu, and Shikoku occupy the main, with their branches, the Kuril Islands in the north, the Ogasawara Islands in the south and Okinawa in the southeast. Japan has many bays and harbors, and the coasts are much indented with violent upheavals and subsidences. Japan is comparatively exposed to disasters by earthquakes, tidal waves or volcanic eruptions because it is subject to violent changes in the earth.

A valley of Mt. Oeyama.

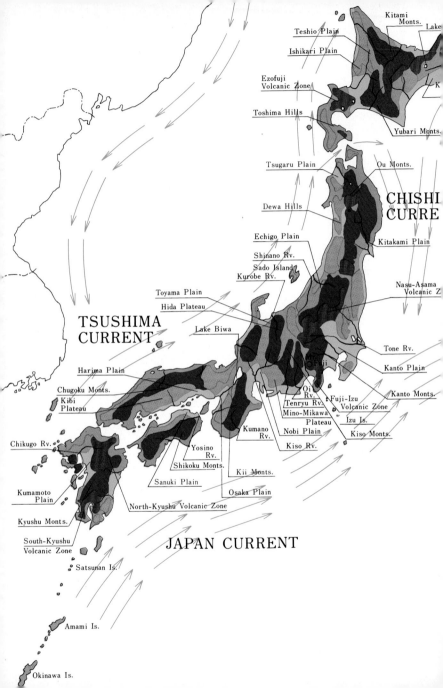

The mountainous province of middle Honshu, called Japan Alps.

POPULATION (1979)

Populations of Major Countries		Population per sq. km.	
China	945,018 X 1,000	Bangladesh	602
India	650,982	South Korea	382
U.S.S.R.	264,108	Holland	344
U.S.A.	220,584	Belgium	322
Indonesia	148,470	Japan	311
Brazil	118,645	Saudi Arabia	4
Japan	115,870	Canada	2
Bangladesh	86,643	Australia	2
West Germany	61,337		

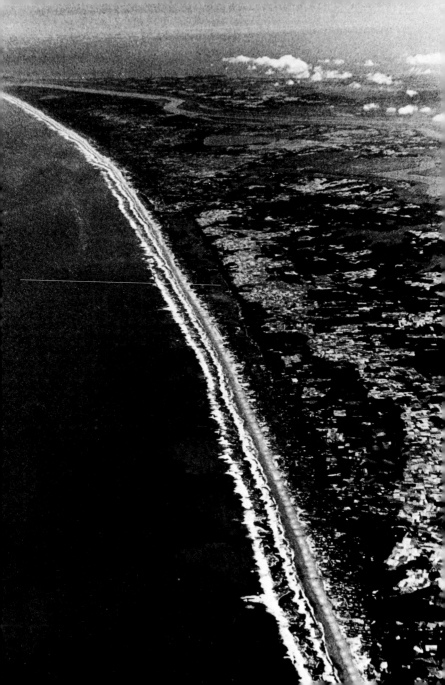

NATIONAL PARKS

Park and Situation   Area

Akan, Hokkaido	90,538	hectare
Daisetsuzan, Hokkaido	230,894	
Shikotsu-Toya, Hokkaido	98,332	
Shiretoko, Hokkaido	39,731	
Towada-Hachimantai, North Honshu	85,409	
Rikuchu Fiord, North Honshu	12,348	
Bandai-Asahi, Middle-North Honshu	189,582	
Nikko, Middle-North Honshu	140,698	
Joshin'etsu Heights, Middle Honshu	189,028	
South Alps, Middle Honshu	35,752	
Chichibu-Tama, Middle Honshu	121,600	
Fuji-Hakone-Izu, East Honshu	123,161	(land covered)
Middle Mountainous Province	169,768	
Hakusan, Middle Honshu	47,683	
Ise-Shima, Mie Pref.	55,550	
Yoshino-Kumano, West-Middle Honshu (Kii Peninsula)	58,546	
San-in Coast, Face to the Japan Sea	8,996	
Daisen-Oki, West Honshu	31,927	
Seto Inland Sea	62,951	(land covered)
Saikai, West Kyushu (Nagasaki Pref.)	24,324	(land covered)
Aso, Middle Kyushu	72,492	
Unzen-Amakusa, West Kyushu	25,496	
Kirishima-Yaku, South Kyushu	54,012	
Iriomote, Okinawa Pref.	12,506	(land covered)
Rishiri-Rebun-Sarobetsu, Hokkaido	21,222	
Ogasawara, Tokyo	6,099	
Ashizuri-Uwami, Shikoku	10,967	

(Left) The linear coast of Kujukuri facing the Pacific Ocean.

ARTS IN LIFE

Tea Ceremony (Sado)

The Japanese began to drink tea in the 6th century A. D., but in those days tea was only an expensive medicine. Later, as it was commonly cultivated, people began to use it as an ordinary beverage. During the Muromachi period the Zen spirit entered the practice of drinking tea.

The originator of tea ceremony is said to be Sen-no Rikyu. In the tea ceremony the beauty of movement was pursued and the form was emphasized. This practice has lasted to this day.

The formal tea ceremony is usually performed in an independent tea-house and is sometimes performed outdoors. Since the primary purpose of the tea ceremony is to make tea and drink it in a quiet manner, we need not overemphasize the elaborate manners, but relax and enjoy ourselves. Several different schools

A scene of a Tea ceremony. The host, left, is preparing the next service and the guest is tasting the green tea.

do exist at present, but their ways of performing the tea ceremony are essentially the same.

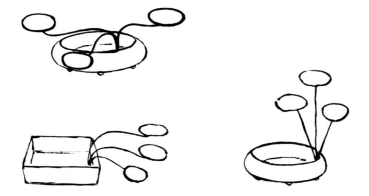

Basic patterns of Flower Arrangement.

Flower Arrangement (Kado)

People all over the world adorn their rooms with pretty flowers. This has been a universal custom since the days of antiquity. In Japan the art of flower arrangement, just like the tea ceremony, was first pursued in the 15th and 16th centuries in accordance with the fundamental laws of Japanese esthetics. It became the highest aim of this art to express the inner life of man by means of flowers and the space they are placed in. The formal laws of the tea ceremony, flower arrangement, landscape gardening, architecture, and artistic handicraft are primarily based on *Furyu-no-michi* or refined accomplishments. Those who were regarded as *Shisho* or masters were generally well acquainted with all those arts.

Today there is even a tendency to go beyond the old formalism and associate the flower arrangement with sculpture as a form of modern art. As in the case of tea ceremony, there are many schools but the fundamentals are almost the same.

A lady in her best kimono is arranging flowers.

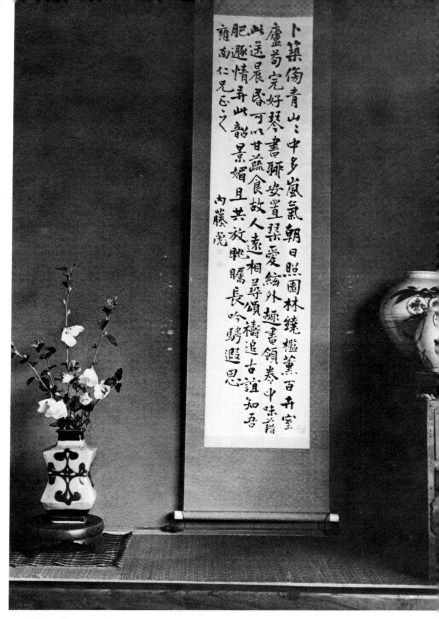

Kakejiku on the wall of *toko-no-ma*, an important corner of traditional houses to appreciate arts.

Calligraphy (Shodo)

A Chinese character is generally made up of a unit of lines symbolizing the shape of an object and an additional unit.

For example —

(sun)	☼	→	⊙	→	日	
(moon)	☽	→	☽	→	月	
(light)	日	＋	月	→	明	

Calligraphy had developed in China before the Christian era and in Japan it flourished with the rise of poetry around the 6th century.

In calligraphy the following three instruments are mainly used —

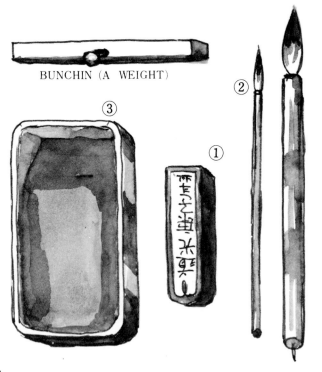

BUNCHIN (A WEIGHT)

② ③ ①

102

1) *Sumi* (an India-ink stick or cake) . . Made by glueing together and hardening the particles of soot from a burnt pinetree.
2) *Fude* (a writing brush) . . A brush made of the hairs of animals like a raccoon which are fastened in a small piece of bamboo.
3) *Suzuri* (an inkstone) . . A solid piece of stone, with a smooth surface, and a dent is for holding water. We produce ink by rubbing the surface with *sumi*.

Towards the end of the 10th century, the Japanese produced the distinct *kana* symbols on the model of the Chinese characters, and developed an entirely different style of calligraphy from the Chinese. Expert calligraphers were ranked with master artists in other fields, and today a history of the fine arts never fails to mention their names and styles of writing. Even at present the calligraphers are regarded as artists. There is now a tendency among calligraphers to approach abstract painting.

TOKAIDO

The name 'Tokaido', which you will often come across, was given in the Edo period to the main route connecting Edo and Kyoto, and means the "Road East" of Kyoto. This old Tokaido Highway extended about 300 miles along the Pacific coast. In the 17th century people walked nearly half a month to cover this distance. Today the 'bullet' trains can make it as far as Osaka in only 3 hours, so most tourists do not have time to enjoy the landscape along the Highway. But there are many spots of scenic beauty, typically Japanese, in this part of Japan. Various kinds of industry also flourish here.

The Meishin Highway ties Nagoya with Osaka and Kobe.

Shizuoka

Leaving Atami, passing through a long tunnel, the bullet train crosses the Fuji-Hakone-Izu Park, and then, passing Mt. Fuji on the right and the shining Suruga Bay on the left, darts down westward.

Along the coast of Suruga Bay the fishing industry is prospering, and you can always see inshore and deep-sea fishing vessels sailing into and out of many ports, such as Numazu, Okitsu, Shimizu, and Yaizu.

Shizuoka is the place where the Shogun Tokugawa Ieyasu spent the one-third of his life, and his ashes are buried in the Kunozan Toshogu Shrine. Nikko Toshogu, though larger, is only its branch-shrine.

In the season of fresh green leaves, you can see people (women) picking tea in this district. Shizuoka also boasts delicious strawberries and oranges.

Young women picking tea leaves.

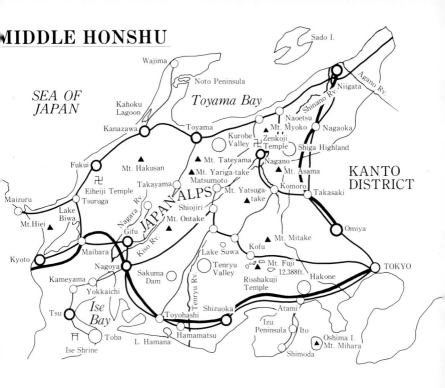

Hamamatsu

The Ooi River and the Tenryu River have their sources in the South Alps. The mountain ranges called by the name of 'Alps' include three groups of high peaks which rise into the clouds like spinal columns in the central areas. These high mountains in central Japan are known as the Japan Alps. This name was first used by William Gowland in his book published in 1881. You can see these peaks, all 9,000 ft. high above sea level, even from the Shinkansen Line 'bullets'.

Situated at the mouth of the Tenryu, Hamamatsu is famous for its musical instrument and automotive industries.

In May it is a custom to fly big kites on the seashore. This is done for the Boys' Festival, to pray to Heaven for their lifelong happiness. The kites are mostly 10 feet in width and length.

107

Blue sky, a red kite with a big white letter on it (left). Carrying a kite, in *happi* coats, children and adults flock from all quarters (below).

Nagoya

Nagoya is reached in 40 minutes from Hamamatsu on the Shinkansen Line. It is the fourth largest city in Japan next to Tokyo, Osaka and Yokohama, and is one of the four major industrial zones in Japan. Chief among the industrial products of Nagoya are automotive vehicles (buses, cars, trucks, etc.), electric appliances and machineries, textile products (a high percentage of the national total), and precision machines (sewing machines and clocks), but most unique must be the production of ceramics.

In Japan the name *setomono* is usually applied to any kind of ceramic ware today, but it literally means 'things (*mono*) from Seto (a city near Nagoya)'. The ceramic output of Nagoya amounts to a high percentage of the total ceramic output of Japan, and 65 per cent of this output is exported. The *Shippoyaki* chinaware or cloisonne is also Nagoya's speciality.

A view of Nagoya Castle.

A scene of the main streets of Nagoya City.

Ise

Let us leave the Shinkansen Line for a while, and visit the eastern parts of the Kii Peninsula.

Yokkaichi City lies across the Kiso River. The city boasts of its petro-chemical *kombinat*.

Sixty miles from Nagoya is Ise City, the seat of Japanese Shintoism. More than 120 shrines surround the Outer and Inner Shrines (the Grand Shrines of Ise). The precincts of the Grand Shrines have a total area of not less than 380 acres, and they are all graveled. It may not be easy to walk on them, especially in high-heeled shoes, but the graveled precincts reflect the wisdom of our ancestors to keep clean and pure the sacred precincts of a shrine.

The two shrines are both entirely built of plain Japanese cypress wood, with big round pillars and thatched roofs. Everything they present is straight and economic, and nothing is a mere ornament. The *Chigi* or cross-beams, which, shaped like the letter 'X', are seen piercing the blue sky, symbolize that God rules heaven and earth.

The architectural style belongs to one of the oldest, but the structures are well balanced and not in the least old-fashioned. The severity of this simple style, asserting that here is the dwelling of the God, seems to deny us human beings our access to it. But even today more than 2,000,000 people visit here every year.

Toba

Another feature of Ise-Shima National Park (which covers the greater part of Ise and Shima provinces) is, needless to say, the Mikimoto pearl farm, which is located near the pier of Toba. Today the name 'Mikimoto' is known to women throughout the world.

The pearl magnate, Kokichi Mikimoto, was born in 1858 of a poor family. At 35, after years of painful labor, he was at last successful in making cultured pearls. He passed away at the age of 95, but the story of his efforts and endurance throughout his life has lived till today, even in school textbooks.

Formerly, the mature pearl oysters were collected by women divers (*Ama*) from the ocean floor, but today the oysters are nurtured in a farm till they are grown. And when they are grown enough, they are hung in the sea from rafts with irritants inserted into them, until pearls grow around the irritants. This is how cultured pearls are made today. It is such a singular view to see those rafts floating in the bays.

Most of the women divers called *Ama,* except the few who work at the pearl farms as a kind of show for the visitors, are now engaged in their primary job, which is to gather other marine products. About 65 per cent of the total marine products of this district (in and near Toba) are obtained yearly by the hands of 1,600 women divers — women aged from 12 to 60 who continue their painful work under the water, wearing white cotton clothes, caps and hydroscopes.

Today the *Ama* work in various places of Japan. Their way of living, being one with Nature, is quite natural in a country surrounded by the sea.

RELIGION

There are three principal religions in Japan, Shintoism, Buddhism, and Christianity.

Shintoism has its origin in the pre-historic ages. It is a system of polytheistic nature worship. The building consecrated to the gods is called a shrine. The close relation of Shintoism and the populace is established in the ceremonies like the wedding, and in the festivals they hold to pray for better harvests or to avoid sickness or calamities.

Buddhism is the religion of India founded by Sakyamuni. It was introduced into Japan through China and Korea in the early 6th century. Buddhism showed a deeper insight into the soul of man and gradually came to pervade the hearts of the common people in a world of continuous battles and revolts. Buddhism is a highly philosophical religion. This is especially true of Zen Buddhism, which was brought into Japan in the early 14th century and has had great influence over the Japanese art in the later ages. It is closely connected with the life of the people chiefly in the funeral rites as a medium through which to pray for the repose of the departed souls. (cf. p. 81)

A Spanish missionary, St. Francis Xavier, visited Japan in 1549 and spread the seeds of Christianity on the Japanese soil. This is the beginning of the Christian religion in our country. Many foreign Catholic priests followed his example, and preached Christianity in Kyushu and Kyoto, but in 1587 a law was issued by Hideyoshi to expel missionaries from Japan. In 1613 a ban was thrown on Christianity, and those who did not convert were either banished to an island or suffered capital punishment. In 1635 commerce with other countries was banned by the Tokugawa Government, and subsequently the Isolation of Japan was completed. It was not until 1873 that Christianity could reassert itself in Japan.

Once it was approved in 1873, it became vigorous again together with European civilization, and today both Catholics and Protestants are engaged in their missionary work with freedom. In addition, there are many Christian schools in Japan today.

Ama (above) and pearl-oyster-rafts at the sunset.

THE JAPAN SEA SIDE DISTRICTS
(Ura Nippon)

The districts on the Japan Sea coast are less developed than those on the Pacific coast. This is mainly because in these areas there is not only a lot of snowfall but there is also only small flat land as the mountains forming the spines of Honshu rise almost right from the sea.

It is in these districts that you can find more of the traditional Japanese ways of living, customs and manners. At the neck of the Noto Peninsula lie two important cities, Toyama and Kanazawa. They each have a long history of 400 years, Toyama as the place where peddlers who sold medicines all over Japan lived, and Kanazawa, once a castle town of prosperous daimios, as a place where industrial art objects were made. Kenroku Park in Kanazawa is considered the first of the Three Beautiful Parks* in Japan.

On the Japan Sea side of the Chugoku district, there are again two old cities—Matsue and Izumo, but Izumo is a place of more historical interest. Izumo is known as one of the cradles of Japanese mythology and has been the seat of many popular beliefs. There is a legend that all the local gods all over the country gather together at Izumo in autumn and stay there for a while. Izumo Taisha has its origin in prehistoric ages. Though the present building was reconstructed in 1744, it has the oldest style of shrine architecture in Japan. Izumo Taisha Shrine is also known as the abode of the god of marriage, and is constantly visited by people who come to spend their honey-moons there. This is because they feel indebted for their marriage to the god's special favor and come to express thanks to him even if they were married in some other place.

* Other two are Korakuen in Okayama, Okayama Pref., and Kairakuen in Mito, Ibaraki Pref.

114

The Kenroku Garden in
Kanazawa City (above).
Izumo Taisha Shrine,
one of the origins of
Japanese Shintoism.

115

Old and young picnicking under cherry blossoms in season.

Gion, city-wide festival of Kyoto, is held in June.
Gorgeous floats called *Yamaboko* are paraded. The
largest float is pulled by 400 men. Other grand
festivals in Kyoto are *Aoi* (May) and *Jidai* (October).
A monarchal procession of the Heian Age is
featured at the former, and the manners and
customs of all ages at Jidai festival.

KYOTO

Kyoto is 40 minutes from Nagoya on the Shinkansen Line. The modern Kyoto Station will be the first to greet you. The long history of Kyoto is not always a mere museum-piece. The traditions Kyoto has are deeply connected with the progressive minds of its people. When the Imperial court, which was the center of Japanese tradition for a long time, transfered to Tokyo, the people started and developed new industries one after another. Paper mills, electrical machinery, textile and other factories began to stand close together. They also started water power generation by utilizing the abundant waters of Lake Biwa, and operated the first steetcar in Japan. It was also in Kyoto that the first department store in Japan was built. The reforming energy that the people of Kyoto showed one hundred years ago at such a turning point of history has lived till today in the minds of the people who are willing to choose a man of progressive ideas as the leader of their government or to receive those professors at Kyoto University who lead the world in theoretical physics.

One hundred years ago the population of Kyoto was only 200,000 and the fact that today it has reached 1,480,044 shows that the city is respectably prospering as a modern city.

Therefore, the numerous old temples that stand here and there in the city are not anachronistic, but show that the people know fully well the importance of preserving what is traditional.

Moreover, it is just surprising that so many ancient Japanese cultural monuments have been preserved till our age, in spite of frequent wars that involved Kyoto during the 1,000 years when it was the capital city of Japan. In no other place can you see so many kinds of the ancient fine arts in so little time as in Kyoto. Kyoto has the one-fourth of all the national treasures of Japan.

The city area of Kyoto has been divided into blocks with straight streets. The streets were first built in the 8th century and run vertically and horizontally throughout the city. Kyoto is a basin, 250 square miles in area, entirely surrounded by hills. The number of the people who visit the city reaches 39,700,000 every year.

The following is the usual course the sightseeing bus starting from Kyoto Station takes in the city.

Higashi- and Nishi-Honganji Temples —— Sanjusangen-doh ("Hall of Thirty-Three Spaces") —— Kiyomizu Temple —— —— Chion-in Temple —— Heian Shrine —— Kinkakuji Temple (Golden Pavilion)

As you see, the places on this course are all temples except the Heian Shrine. The more complicated course only covers a larger number of the temples. But these temples are not the only spots of interest. The popular spots besides them include beautiful Arashiyama Park, Gosho or the old Imperial Palace of Kyoto, Gion, the town famed for its festival, and Lake Biwa in the suburbs, the largest lake in Japan.

Kinkakuji Temple (Golden Pavilion)

A three-storied building stands in a pond called Kyoko-ike or 'Lake of Mirrors'. The building is surrounded by a garden where many trees grow as in the deep woods. The second and the third stories are gilded all over. This building is the Kinkakuji Temple, the "Temple of the Golden Pavilion." This temple was first built in 1397 as a villa of the then Shogun, Ashikaga Yoshimitsu, but was unfortunately burnt down in July, 1950. Five years later, however, an exact replica of the old building was erected, so that Kyoto has been saved from losing an old idol of thousands of people.

Kiyomizu Temple

This temple stands on a cliff. It has a wooden platform in front, supported by a scaffold made by joining big timbers together. This platform is usually called *Kiyomizu-no Butai,* or "Kiyomizu Stage." From this *Butai* you can enjoy a wonderful

Saihoji Temple is known as the "Moss" Temple.

A bird's - eye view of snowy Heian Shrine.

view of the city. Kiyomizu Temple was built in the 8th century and is one of the oldest temples in Kyoto. It was reconstructed in 1630. When they reconstruct any building, the Japanese usually try to keep it as it has been to the best of their abilities. This may do credit to their character.

The district around the temple is noted for the production of earthenware called *Kiyomizu Yaki*. The road leading down to the city is known as "Teapot Lane" among foreign visitors.

Ryoanji Temple

Ryoanji is famous for its unique garden. Known as the 'Rock Garden', this garden is the best specimen of the gardens classified as Karesansui Teien or 'Dried-up Landscape Gardens'. It was constructed probably about 1450. Occupying an area of 500 square feet, it is rectangular in form and is surrounded by white earthen walls on three sides and abuts on a temple building on the last one side.

The building is called *Hojo* (the place where the elder priest of a temple lives). The garden is graveled all over with white sand, and has geometrical furrows (straight or circular) on it. This represents the sea. The 15 stones skillfully arranged represent so many islands. The stones are arranged in such a way that one of them may be concealed when seen from within the *Hojo*.

While many attempts have been made to explain this rock garden, which is said to symbolize the truth of Zen Buddhism, it is certain that you can feel in the simplicity of this garden the oneness of man with all things.

Heian Shrine

Built in 1895 in commemoration of the 1,100th anniversary of the establishment of Kyoto as the Capital of Japan, this shrine, compared with other temples and shrines, is quite modern. But foreign visitors are attracted by its Chinese-style building, free and easy and painted in bright scarlet. Many Japanese regard it rather as a wedding hall.

Heian, which means 'peace and tranquility', is the oldest name of Kyoto.

Next to the Heian Shrine is Okazaki Park, in which there are such public establishments as a zoo, a public hall, and a library.

Highschool students are busy visiting temples and other 'musts' in Kyoto on their school excursion (above).

New Kyoto Station, back, and the old pagoda of Toji Temple.

123

A show window of a shop selling only fans for hundreds years in Kyoto.

Kyoto International Conference Hall

The Hall was built in May, 1966, by the Takara pond (Takaraga-Ike), at the foot of a mountain not too far from the city area. It provides a hall for international conferences. It is the largest of its kind next to the Palais de Nations of Geneva and the U. N. Building of New York City. The combination of the letter 'V' and the inverted 'V' forms resembles the traditional Japanese style found in the roofs of farm-houses in a mountainside village.

Kyoto International Conference Hall, and interior of it (next page).

125

The Katsura Imperial Villa

Built in the 7th century, the Katsura Imperial Villa is the most artistic ancient building in Japan. The villa reflects the mind of harmoney. The material and its form, function and beauty, and art and nature—all these become one in this building. It is a pity that we cannot see it without permission.

The Honganji Temples

The Honganji Temples are the headquarters of the Jodo-Shin Sect, which has the largest number of followers in Japan today. The Honganji Temples are two: one is Higashi or East Honganji, and the other Nishi or West Honganji. They have 16,000,000 adherents today. The reason why there are two temples of the same sect is that in the Edo period Tokugawa Ieyasu separated all religious groups lest they should have a greater influence.

The Higashi Honganji Temple faces the entrance of the Main Street of the city and is situated, among other temples, at the shortest distance from Kyoto Station. The Founder's Hall, 211 feet in length and 191 feet in width, is very beautiful, with its roofs slanting massively. Numbers of doves alight on the precincts, and court the visitors' favor.

The Nishi Honganji Temple is located close by. It is the treasure-house of the works of art of the Momoyama period.

Both temples are quite interested in training young priests, and run a Buddhist university and various kinds of schools.

Daigoji Samboin Temple

The Samboin Temple stands in the mountain 3 miles from Kyoto Station. It was founded in 874 and is one of the oldest temples in Kyoto. The Samboin was originally only an attached temple but today it has become an independant and central one of Daigoji. The beautiful garden was made in 1252 at the will of Toyotomi Hideyoshi. Hideyoshi had ruled Japan as a great generalissimo in a period of wars and revolts until his clan was defeated by Ieyasu. More than 700 stones were donated from all over the country for the laying out of the garden. But Hideyoshi could not live to see the completed garden.

Higashi Honganji Temple in winter.

Daigoji Samboin Temple.

Fushimi Inari Shrine

This shrine is dedicated to *Inari* or the God of Harvest. It is commonly believed that the fox is the God's messenger. The *Inari* worship is the most flourishing in Japan.

Every *Inari* shrine has a gate painted in Chinese red. The Fushimi Inari Shrine has some 20,000 gates of this kind, and when you walk through them you feel as if you were passing through a red tunnel.

Gosho (The Old Imperial Palace)

Gosho, the old Imperial Palace, is situated in the center of the city. Nobody can enter it without permission. Even today the Coronation ceremony is performed at this Palace, in a conspicuous building called Shishinden. A cherry-tree is planted on the eastern side of the entrance, and on the western side a citrus tree. The cherry tree is a symbol of loyalty and the citrus tree symbolizes eternity.

A building called Seiryoden was intended as a living room for emperors. It well preserves an architectural style called Shinden-zukuri, which means the 'style of residence for the nobility'.

Nijo Castle

Nijo Castle was completed in 1603. Being built on flat land, it is a castle in name, for it was in fact a villa of the Tokugawa Shogunate, not a building for battle.

Everybody can enter the castle. You can see the beautiful *fusuma-e* (the sliding-door picture) painted by artists of the Kano school. *Fusuma* is a kind of movable wooden partition of a room with sheets of paper pasted on it. Every Japanese house has this kind of wooden partition. It may be called 'a movable wall'.

To get back to the city, the moment you turn from the main streets where modern buildings and houses stand close together, you find old houses with old lattice doors. These are the common houses in Kyoto which retain the 17th century style just as it was. In a district called Gion (synonym for Yasaka Shrine), you will sometimes be surprised to see dancing girls (Maiko) appear in fascinating dresses from behind the old dark doors. These dancing girls lead a disciplined life in order to master the traditional art of singing and dancing and playing musical instruments.

Since there are only 40 of them now, it is not too much to say that they live but in our imagination. But they are the only people that inherit the traditional art of dancing and singing. They never fail to keep in shape the *kimono* and *obi* they wear.

For the sightseeing tourists, the Maiko will perform an ancient dance at where they stay.

Every old house in Kyoto is unique in structure. It has a great depth, though the dark doorway facing the street is quite narrow. Sometimes, when you follow a passage on the earth floor (*doma*) of the house, you can find a bright modern room at the end of the passage. This kind of combination of old and new styles of living is a product of the wisdom of the people of Kyoto, the city which experienced conflicts and battles during the greater part of its long history.

The whole area south of Kyoto Station is a district of industrial factories. Various alcoholic beverages are brewed or distilled in this district. Excellent *sake* and whisky are produced here mainly because a good quality of water is obtainable just as in and near Kobe.

Lake Biwa

Spreading to the north-east of Kyoto, Lake Biwa is the largest lake in Japan. In ancient times the lake was said to have been connected with the Inland Sea. It has an expanse of 1,700 acres. The lake is so named because it resembles in shape a musical instrument called *Biwa*.

132

"Rock Garden" of Ryoanji Temple (above).
Patterns of Biwa. Fish along the straight row of mesh, and are at last corraled in the smallest crescent trap (below).

ZEN

Zen Buddhism was first impersonated by Bodhidharma in India in the early 6th century. Bodhidharma was one of the twenty-eight founders who strived to understand the teaching of Sakyamuni Gautama and prove it upon their pulses. Therefore Zen is not a school or division of Buddhism but must be that which teaches the fundamental principles of Buddhism. Zen was first introduced into Japan in the 7th century, and spread over the country in the 12th.

Zen Buddhism consists in the intuition through experience. It was the late Daisetsu Suzuki that did his best to teach Zen to people all over the world. In his books you will come across such essential words as *Daichi* ('transcendental wisdom') and *Daihi* ('love or compassion'). Behind these words is the philosophical proposition that man is naturally a free existence. The important thing is that we should not wait for someone to teach us what such words imply but try to grasp it for ourselves and be free ourselves.

Zen has had great influence upon various aspects of Japanese culture. Its influence has extended to the fine arts (especially, water-color painting), *Kendo,* tea ceremony, calligraphy, flower arrangement, *haiku,* and gardening. It may be interesting to note that Zen has contributed greatly to the spiritual formation of the samurai (Japanese warrior). The samurai learned from Zen not only the moral code but also the habit of contemplating upon life and death.

The samurai was originally a fighting employee who was subject to the lord, but later the name *samurai* came to be applied to all the intellectuals.

There are many ways of the practice of Zen, but the most well known is Za-zen. In the practice of Za-zen it is necessary to sit cross-legged in meditation, keeping the body straight from the waist upward, and to make an effort to throw away all worldly thoughts.

Dr. Daisetsu Suzuki. (1870-1966)

A front view of gigantic Daibutsuden Hall of Todaiji Temple.

137

NARA

Being the oldest capital of Japan, Nara is the city the Japanese are led to think of as their home. Even today the relics of an ancient city are found in Nara, situated in the basin about 24 miles to the south of Kyoto and surrounded by low hills. The large tombs of emperors stand just like hills. There are also several stony vestiges of the ancient age.

Nara had been the greatest and most beautiful town in Japan from the end of the 6th century, when Buddhism was introduced from India, till 784, the year when the capital was transfered from Nara.

The days were that able men helped the empress to govern the country. Among those men, Prince Shotoku (whose portrait is printed on the present Japanese notes) played an important role in improving the politics and in encouraging education until his death in 621.

In his age, which is known as the Nara period, the unity of Japan was accomplished for the first time, and the young men absorbed the civilizations of the more advanced nations, China and Korea, as they grew up.

What we feel proud of is rather that we have preserved the relics of this ancient culture. The five-storied pagoda of Horyuji Temple was erected in 607 A.D., and so, as it still stands today, it has survived over an unbelievable period of time in spite of its wooden structure. The temple is also the oldest wooden structure in the world. It must have been quite fortunate for the entire world that such ancient cities as Nara and Kyoto escaped the Second World War.

Todaiji Temple

Todaiji Temple was the seat of Buddhism and general culture in the Nara period. The buildings which you can see today were those reconstructed in 1913 after the old ones were destroyed by frequent wars, but it is not impossible to imagine the glory of the temple. The Great South Entrance, Nigatsu-doh (the February Hall), Sangatsu-doh (the March Hall), Kaidan-in Hall, and the old images of Buddha kept within these buildings—to explain about all of them is impossible in a limited space. Therefore, let us see only the *Daibutsu* or Great Buddha which is the most loved by the Japanese.

Daibutsu

The greatest bronze image of Buddha in the world was cast in 752 A.D., about the time when in Europe the Saracens were increasing greater strength and in Asia China was the power that could vie with the Saracens.

By that time the unity of Japan had been accomplished, and the Imperial Court magnified the central power. The Imperial Court in those days was not the symbol of the nation as it is today, but actually the center of the government. Emperor Seimu was the first to suggest that Daibutsu be constructed. It is to be remembered that the Emperor deeply sympathized with the newest idea of the day, namely, the Buddhist idea of the fusion of one with the many, that all things are related to all other things, and his dream for a statue of Buddha was finally realized by the tears and sweat of over 420,000 men.

The Todaiji Temple was burnt twice since the foundation of the Image, but the Image was twice restored. Just as the archibishop Gyoki gave instruction to the people in first constructing the temple throughout his life, so in reconstructing it many people worked hard under the direction of a devoted leader.

Today a huge statue of Buddha 171 feet in height and 452 tons in weight—an image of *Vairocana* or Buddha, which is worshiped by the Kegon Sect—gives blessings to every visitor, with a quiet expression on its face. We are not boasting only of the size of the Daibutsu or its dwelling, the Daibutsu-den Hall (height—160 feet; frontage—187 feet; side—166 feet. The largest wooden structure in the world).

In 1973 Showa Era's Large Repair Program was started, and it was successfully accomplished on September 30, 1980. On October 15, 1980, the completion ceremony was held.

A finger of the Daibutsu is as large as a man. Width of eyes
is 3 ft. 9 in., and height of face, 16 ft.

Horyuji Temple

What is to be said about every old temple in Japan is that the older the temple is the more it shows of the influences of the ages it has gone through. Horyuji Temple, however, retains the oldest style of temple architecture in Japan. The Five-Storied Pagoda, Kon-doh Hall, the Scripture Museum, the Treasure Museum, and the beautifully named Yumedono Chapel or Dream Hall (which houses the Guze Kan-non Image, first made public in 1884 by Fenollosa, American Orientalist)—the 33 buildings including those just mentioned were constructed over a long period of time extending from 552 to 1868.

Horyuji Temple is situated in the suburbs of Nara City. It is 12 miles from Todaiji Temple. The vicinity is a perfect rural landscape, which would seem to have made no change at all during these 1,300 years.

Kasuga Taisha Shrine

This shrine painted in bright vermillion, looks conspicuous in an old town which has a simple but refined tone of color. The shrine was built by the Fujiwara Clan who were the most influential in the 11th century. The Fujiwaras were, like the Shogunate in the later days, the actual rulers of Japan.

Most interesting will be the stone lanterns, about 3,000 in number, standing on both sides of the approach to the colorful shrine and some bronze lanterns hanging from the roof. These lanterns were all donated by the people who were under the rule of the Fujiwaras. They are lit to shine beautifully twice a year.

The Deer

Occupying an area of 1,250 acres, Nara Park adjoins the Kasuga Shrine and is famous for its numerous deer roaming about in it, which are regarded as the divine messengers of the Shrine. Since there is nobody who will do harm to the sacred deer, they are not afraid of men at all. They are so lovely that they can take their favorite *senbei* (rice-crackers) from the visitor's hands.

141

Horyuji Temple. Kondo Hall, left, and famous *Goju-no Toh,*
five-storied pagoda. (above)
Visitors from abroad love to feed deer in Nara Park. (right)

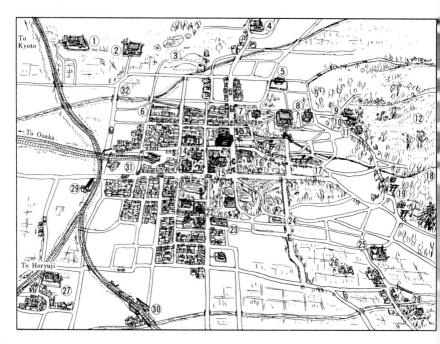

1.	Futaiji Temple	17.	Nara Park
2.	Konbu-in	18.	Kasuga Hill
3.	Hill-like Tombs of Emperor	19.	Kasuga Taisha Shrine
	Shomu and of his Consort	20.	Sarusawa Pond
4.	Hannyaji Temple	21.	Nara Hotel
5.	Shoso-in	22.	City Office
6.	Nara Women's Univ.	23.	Jurin-in Temple
7.	Kaidan-in	24.	Tatchu
8.	Todaiji Temple	25.	Shin-Yakushiji Temple
9.	Nigatsu-doh	26.	Nara Gakugei Univ.
10.	Sangatsu-doh	27.	Daianji Temple
11.	Tamuke-yama Shrine	28.	Byakugoji Temple
12.	Wakakusa Hill	29.	Nara Station of the Japanese
13.	Prefectural Office		National Railways.
14.	Kofukuji Temple	30.	Kyobate Stn. of JNR
15.	Five Storied Pagoda	31.	Nara Stn. of KNR
16.	Museum	32.	Saho Rv.

Horyuji overlooked.

TRADITIONAL AMUSEMENTS

Noh and Kyogen

Noh and Kyogen plays are forms of theatrical art which were brought to a culmination during the Muromachi period. The two dramatic forms evolved originally from *Sarugaku* and other religious songs and dances, such as *Kagura* (the Shinto god dance), *Dengaku* (primitive ritual dance among the farmers), *Gigaku* (ancient Indian morality dance), *Bugaku* (Korean song and dance), and *Gagaku* (banquet music in China during the Tang dynasty).

A form of esoteric Buddhist rituals in origin, the *Sarugaku* became a dramatic performance that could stand appreciation in the Heian and Kamakura periods. In the Kamakura period it became more spiritual and Yugenistic under the influence of Buddhism, especially the Jishu Sect, and came to be represented by *Noh*. Although the comical elements of *Sarugaku* existed as *Kyogen, Noh* became an independent dramatic performance, including songs and dances.

The *Noh* play was popular among the upper classes including noblemen, Buddhist priests, and warriors, while the *Kyogen* was fostered by the middle class. Though the *Noh* and the *Kyogen* are separate in essence, they are often performed together. The *Kyogen* is staged only during an interval between the acts of the *Noh* play for the purpose of entertaining the audience, but nowadays it has been re-evaluated as a form of comedy full of sharp criticisms and is ranked with the *Noh* play.

There are at present five schools of *Noh* (*Kanze, Hosho, Kongo, Kita,* and *Konparu*) and three in *Kyogen* (*Okura, Izumi,* and *Sagi*).

In *Noh* and *Kyogen* the principal actors wear masks, as in classical Greek dramas, but in the case of the Japanese plays the masks are used to symbolize the sex, age, personality and social status of a character and are evaluated as works of art.

Kabuki

About 1600, a woman named O-kuni, who was in the service of a shrine, got together a troupe of dancers and used to run a show on the Kamo River in Kyoto City. This was the beginning of the history of *Kabuki*. In 1630 the government prohibited women from appearing on the stage to control immoral practices. Consequently, a man had to play a woman's part, and as much art was needed to do so, there appeared male actors known as *Oyama,* who specialized in playing the roles of female characters of a *Kabuki* play. Even today women do not appear on the *Kabuki* stage.

From 1688 to 1704, Edo culture flourished remarkably, and in the field of *Kabuki* the acting editions were greatly improved. The actors trained to express complicated feelings, and the art of performance strictly formalized. In those days the Kabuki circles were divided into two, one being Kyoto and Osaka, the other Edo. Kyoto and Osaka produced famous tragedies and comedies, while stormy plays were born in Edo.

Although many of the *Kabuki* plays were at first adapted from *Noh* dramas and *Bunraku* (a puppet show flourishing in 17~18th century), original writings came to be created for the *Kabuki* stage. The latter half of the 17th century witnessed the appearance of the playwrights who wrote tragedies based on incidents in everyday life. Chikamatsu Monzaemon is the most distinguished of these playwrights, and is highly evaluated today.

With something of a formalized musical play, the *Kabuki* drama includes everything required in dramatic art, and has won a universal reputation as a theatrical art grown from Japanese soil.

Bon-Odori (Bon Folk Dance)

Bon Odori is a kind of folk dance performed all over the country during the Bon period (*see* p. 81). Dating from the early 14th century, it has become very popular as an occasion to dance a summer night away to the accompaniment of folk songs. There is a great variety of Bon Odori, but generally people dance at temples or in the open fields around a scaffold on which the musicians are seated. The well-known Awa-Odori of Shikoku is so lively that it fills the streets with an atmosphere of a great festival, with the people dancing it freely in their own ways.

Incidentally, the Japanese residents in America hold Bon Festival Dance every year at Riverside Park in New York.

147

The Matsukaze, a Noh drama, on stage. Actors
wear masks and musicians with choir are seated
on the same stage floor.

A make-up of Kabuki actor.

A stage of *Bunraku*.

A chinaware bazaar in Osaka.

150

OSAKA

Osaka dates from about the 4th century as a seaport town. Toward the end of the 15th century Ishiyama Temple was erected on the site where the present Osaka Castle stands. In times of war, a group of Buddhists took up arms and fortified themselves in this temple. Afterwards, Toyotomi Hideyoshi had a castle built there, and from this time on until Tokugawa Ieyasu took over the government in 1596, Osaka City remained the center of foreign trade, especially with China. Many merchants gathered at Osaka, and their commercial spirit came to have them called "Osaka Merchants." Their spirit has remained alive till this day, and has made Osaka the second largest city in Japan.

Osaka is located at the mouth of the Yodogawa River. The watercourses run in all directions throughout the city. The total length is 110 miles and occupies 12 per cent of the total area of the city. This is why the city is called "Mizuno Miyako" (City of Water). The population is 2,623,123. Osaka and the surrounding cities including Kobe are crowded with cotton spinning and chemical fiber factories. These districts possess 40 per cent of fiber factory workers in Japan. Osaka has made a great development in pharmaceutical industry and its production accounts for a fairly large share of the total amount of medicines in Japan.

As a matter of fact, there is only one thing in the industrial city Osaka that can attract a sightseeing tourist. It is the Osaka Castle. This castle, completed in 1585, was in those days the largest and strongest fortress in the country. Tokugawa Ieyasu attacked the Toyotomis at this castle, but he was checked by the water moats and the strong walls surrounding the castle, so that he could at last capture it only by having the moats reclaimed by means of stratagems. The present site reveals only a small portion of its original area of 274 acres, but nevertheless the castle boasts the 135-foot-high donjon (Tower-Keep, reconstructed 1931) and the 45-foot-high stone walls. Among the stones used for making the walls there is a huge one measuring 47.6 feet in width and 19.2 feet in height.

A view of
Shinsaibashi,
Osaka

153

In 1970 the International Exposition was held at the Senri Hills, about six miles north-east of downtown Osaka. It was the first full-scale world exposition held in Asia, and its theme was entitled "Progress and Harmony for Mankind." There were 77 different countries which participated and over 50 million people visited the event during its six-months run.

Formerly the EXPO'70 site was a rural area of pine-clad slopes and ravines terraced for rice paddies. However, serious study has been given on how to preserve the 3.5 million square metre site to serve as an example of the integrated design that will be needed to make large Japanese cities pleasant places in which to live. Now, Senri Hills is a landscape guide of the future for Japan.

KOBE

Kobe as well as Osaka has long been an important seaport in Japan. Kobe Harbor was first opened for foreign trade in 1867. Today it has a mooring capacity for scores of vessels. The results of 1976 showed that exports were at 24,240,000 tons, 20.8 per cent of the total amount of Japan, and imports 20,920,000 tons, 5.9 per cent of the country's total. The relation between Kobe and Osaka is similar to that between Tokyo and Yokohama.

Mt. Rokko, 3,000 feet high, rises behind Kobe City, and checks the inflow of cold air from the north, creating a mild climate in this district.

Kobe is famous not only for its trading port, but also for its many industries, such as shipbuilding, metal manufacturing, rubber goods manufacturing, machinery manufacturing, and chemical industry, which are all prospering. Factories number more than 4,000. Kobe is also noted for its *sake* brewing and match manufacturing.

In March 1981 "Portpia" was held with many events. After that, in October of that year, the same site was reopened to the general public as "Port Island" serving as a pleasant place for recreation.

154

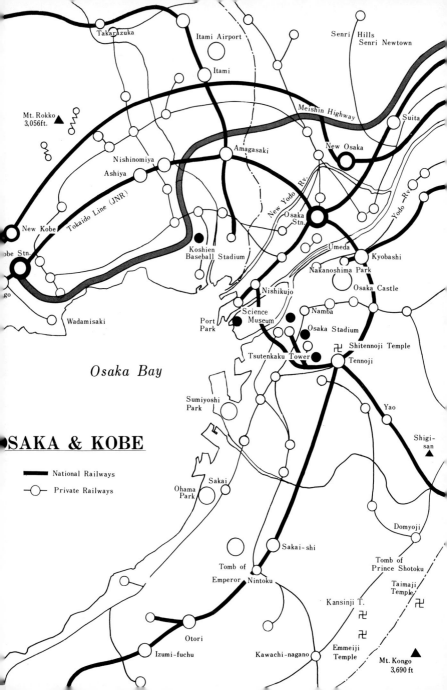

Takarazuka

Itami Airport

Itami

Senri Hills
Senri Newtown

Mt. Rokko
3,056ft.

Meishin Highway

Suita

New Osaka

Nishinomiya

Ashiya

Amagasaki

New Yodo Rv.

Osaka
Stn.

Yodo Rv.

New Kobe

Tokaido Line (JNR)

obe Stn.

go

Koshien
Baseball Stadium

Umeda

Kyobashi

Nakanoshima Park

Osaka Castle

Nishikujo

Wadamisaki

Namba

Science
Museum

Port
Park

Osaka Stadium

Shitennoji Temple

Tsutenkaku Tower

Tennoji

Osaka Bay

Sumiyoshi
Park

Yao

Shigi-
san

SAKA & KOBE

— National Railways
—○— Private Railways

Ohama
Park

Sakai

Domyoji

Sakai-shi

Tomb of
Prince Shotoku

Tomb of
Emperor Nintoku

Taimaji
Temple

Kansinji T.

Otori

Izumi-fuchu

Kawachi-nagano

Emmeiji
Temple

Mt. Kongo
3,690 ft

The huge tomb of Emperor Nintoku, constructed in the 5 or 6th century, is in Sakai
City near Osaka. Three moats surround the
hill-like tomb of 475 meters in length and
300 in width, three times larger than the
biggest pyramid in area.

Twilight on the Inland Sea (Seto-naikai). (right)

THE INLAND SEA OF JAPAN

Just as the ancient European civilizations flourished in the Mediterranean region, so the cradle of the Japanese civilization was along the Inland Sea coast, about 1,500 years ago, the Inland Sea served as an important commercial route connecting Nara, the seat of the Imperial Court, and the Kyushu district, which was the gate to China and Korea. In this sea, separating Shikoku from western Honshu, there are over 300 islands, large and small, presenting a beautiful view. The Inland Sea is one of the earliest to have been given the name of the National Park in Japan. The navigation route connecting Kobe and Beppu (in Kyushu) threads its course among the small islands. And now, you can go to Hiroshima, Okayama and Fukuoka by the Shinkansen Line.

The Himeji Castle.

CITIES ON THE INLAND SEA COAST

Himeji

Himeji is 30 miles from Kobe. The city possesses the Himeji Castle, the most beautiful and largest that can be seen in Japan. Shirasagi (White Heron) Castle, synonym for Himeji Castle, is a name worthy of its graceful white fortress. The many-storied castle has escaped fire, and retains its valiant figure just as it was in the 14th century.

Kurashiki

In the Edo period Kurashiki City was under the direct control of the Bakufu (Shogunate Government). This is because the city was the distribution center of rice in this part of Japan. In one area of the city, which is becoming more modern day by day, are seen the storehouses with white plastered walls, producing a quiet atmosphere. Magosaburo Ohara, who had achieved success in his spinning industry, had a picture gallery built here, and made public his collection of masterpieces of the world, such as by Greco, Cézanne, Pissaro, Degas, Monet, and Rouault. This is the forerunner of the kind of picture gallery which collects European works of art in Japan.

Takamatsu

Takamatsu City is the gateway of Shikoku to Honshu, the Main Island. In the 12th century, the last battle of the largest civil war in Japan was fought in and around the Inland Sea, and so there are many things in Takamatsu that preserve traces of this ancient battle.

Tokushima, situated 25 miles to the east of Takamatsu, is famous for its Awa Folk Dance, which is performed by all the people every summer.

The Inland Sea coasts are prospering in *tai* fishing. The *tai* (sea-bream) is regarded as the noblest kind of fish in Japan.

Enthusiasm! Awa Folk Dance attracts some
3,000,000 people within four nights sequence.

The Atom-bombed Dome, front, and the Park of Peace, Hiroshima. In the flat building above are many articles and reminders of the tragedy.

Hiroshima

Hiroshima has come to be recorded forever in the history of mankind as the city destroyed by the first atomic bomb ever used in the world.

In the explosion center a ruined building called "Atom-Bombed Dome" is still preserved today, but the city has completely become a place fit for men to live in. In its outward appearance, at least, Hiroshima is developing in the same way as other cities.

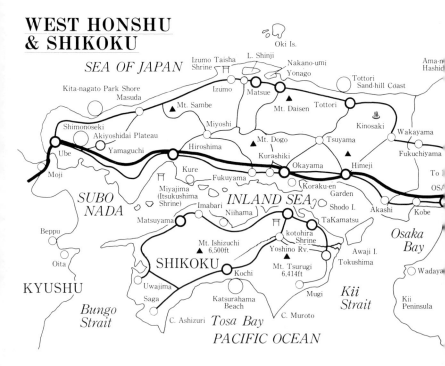

WEST HONSHU
& SHIKOKU

SEA OF JAPAN

Oki Is.

Izumo Taisha
Shrine

L. Shinji

Nakano-umi
Yonago

Ama-n
Hashid

Kita-nagato Park Shore
Masuda

Izumo

Matsue

Tottori
Sand-hill Coast

Mt. Sambe

Mt. Daisen

Tottori

Shimonoseki

Miyoshi

Kinosaki

Wakayama

Akiyoshidai Plateau

Mt. Dogo

Tsuyama

Ube

Yamaguchi

Hiroshima

Kurashiki

Fukuchiyama

Moji

Kure

Okayama

Himeji

To

Fukuyama

Koraku-en
Garden

OSA

Miyajima
(Itsukushima
Shrine)

INLAND SEA

Shodo I.

Akashi

Kobe

*SUBO
NADA*

Imabari

Niihama

TaKamatsu

Beppu

Matsuyama

kotohira
Shrine

*Osaka
Bay*

Mt. Ishizuchi
▲ 6,500ft

Yoshino Rv.

Awaji I.

Oita

SHIKOKU

Mt. Tsurugi
6,414ft

Tokushima

Wadaya

Kochi

KYUSHU

Uwajima

Mugi

*Kii
Strait*

Kii
Peninsula

Saga

Katsurahama
Beach

*Bungo
Strait*

C. Ashizuri

C. Muroto

Tosa Bay

PACIFIC OCEAN

Steam of spas in Beppu.

KYUSHU

By the Shinkansen Line you can get to Kyushu in 7 hours from Tokyo, passing through the Kanmon Tunnel, and by airplane you can come to this "southern country"of Japan in only 2or 3 hours. The southern tip of Kyushu is in the same latitude as the Florida Peninsula in America. In the sea surrounding the island flows a warm current. You can see tropical plants, and strange customs and manners here and there in Kyushu.

Beppu

The city of hot springs. There are about 3,500 hot springs in the city. The hot water of Beppu is especially noted for its high medicinal value. In the suburbs there stands a low mountain called Mt. Takasaki, where wild monkeys live in crowds. (Through a study of the wild monkeys primatology, a credit to Japan, has been established.) Highways starting at Beppu extend to every part of Kyushu. One of them runs through the Aso National Park and reaches Kumamoto.

Hellish crater of Mt. Aso.

Aso

A large mountain district, 277 square miles in area, has been designated a National Park. The district include the volcanic zones of Mt. Aso and Mt. Kuju (5,900 feet high; the highest in Kyushu). The surprisingly large crater-basin is the focus of a distant view. This crater-basin, 48 miles in circumference, is a tableland of volcanic ashes and pasture, where several towns are and 80,000 people are living. There are also five railway stations and five peaks, each more than 4,300 feet high. The peak which still ejects smoke and steam is Mt. Nakadake, which is 4,335 feet above the sea level.

Nagasaki

Historically, Nagasaki is an old seaport. Even under the policy of isolation in the Edo period, only Nagasaki had commerce with Holland and China, so that today things in Nagasaki retain

The boundless expanse of a crater-basin called *Kusasenri.*

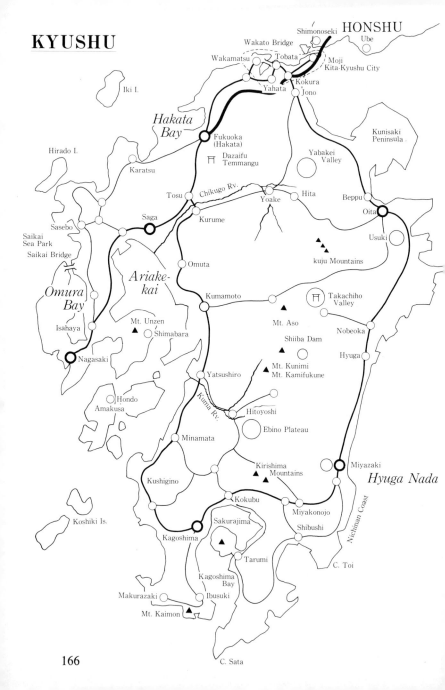

KYUSHU

HONSHU

Shimonoseki
Ube
Wakato Bridge
Wakamatsu
Tobata
Moji
Kita-Kyushu City
Kokura
Yahata
Jono

Iki I.

Hakata Bay

Fukuoka (Hakata)

Kunisaki Peninsula

Dazaifu Temmangu
Yabakei Valley

Hirado I.

Karatsu

Tosu
Chikugo Rv.
Yoake
Hita
Beppu

Saga
Kurume
Oita

Sasebo
Usuki

Saikai Sea Park
Saikai Bridge

Ariake-kai

Omuta

kuju Mountains

Omura Bay

Isahaya

Mt. Unzen
Shimabara

Kumamoto

Takachiho Valley

Mt. Aso

Shiiba Dam

Nobeoka

Nagasaki

Yatsushiro

Mt. Kunimi
Mt. Kamifukune

Hyuga

Hondo
Amakusa

Kuma Rv.
Hitoyoshi

Ebino Plateau

Minamata

Kirishima Mountains

Miyazaki

Hyuga Nada

Kushigino

Kokubu

Miyakonojo

Koshiki Is.

Sakurajima

Shibushi

Kagoshima

Tarumi

Nichinan Coast

C. Toi

Makurazaki
Ibusuki

Kagoshima Bay

Mt. Kaimon

C. Sata

vivid influences of these two countries. The city even preserves an all Chinese style temple called Kara Dera (Tang Temple).

Nagasaki and the adjoining areas were the places that witnessed the sufferings of the Christians in Japan. In 1597 twenty-six Roman Catholic believers (known as the "26 Saints of Japan") were executed on crosses, and since then Christianity was long cruelly suppressed by the Toyotomi and the Tokugawa families. It was only in 1864 that a cathedral was built at Oura in Nagasaki, but at last the Christian life, which long had to be kept secret, could see the light of day.

In 1945 a second atomic bomb following the first one on Hiroshima was dropped on Nagasaki. The people's suffering might have been comparable to that during the long history of persecution of Christianity in the city.

With the many slopes seen in the city, Nagasaki can also offer an exotic atmosphere for Japanese and foreign visitors alike.

In Nagasaki there is the largest dockyard in the world, Mitsubishi Dockyard, which has an average shipbuilding capacity of 3,818,782 gross tons Dwt. a year. And Sasebo, located 12 miles from Nagasaki, was once and is now a city resembling a naval port in character. The reason why an atomic bomb was dropped not on these important areas but on a cathedral, the seat of religion, is only, it is said, that the sky chanced to be cloudless just above there.

The Five Bridges of Amakusa

The coast-lines in the southern parts of Kyushu are crooked and complicated. The sea is smooth and calm like a lake on a windless day. The numerous islands resemble Japanese gardens so much that they look somehow artificial. In 1966 several of the islands were connected by bridges. Especially beautiful is the Saikai Bridge built over the rapid current of Omura Bay. The Saikai National Park ranks beside the Inland Sea National Park as the most beautiful 'sea park' in Japan.

Five bridges of Amakusa binding tiny green islets.

The Wakato Bridge combining Wakamatsu
and Tobata in Kita-kyushu City (above left).
Eternal prayers. The memorial of 26 Martyrs,
Nagasaki (below left).

Sakurajima

Sakurajima is a volcanic island situated in the bosom of Kagoshima Bay, to the east of Kagoshima City, the largest city in the south of Japan. It still ejects white smoke, and the destructive power that its beautiful figure keeps within is frequently compared to the passion of women in the southern regions of Japan. In 1914, the year of the outbreak of World War I, Sakurajima burst into eruption so violently that the island became connected by lava with the main island of Kyushu.

Kita-kyushu City

In 1963 five cities in Kyushu were united as an industrial city with a population of 1,063,990. This is the City of Kita-kyushu. It is a city of iron foundries, including Nippon Steel Corporation. This city is noted for its many industries, such as shipbuilding, cement and marine product industries. The symbol of this young city in the north of Kyushu is the Wakato Great Bridge. Pedestrians use an elevator at the foot of the bridge to cross it.

OKINAWA

General

Okinawa is the main island of the subtropical Ryukyu chain, and its outstanding features are its southern climate, crystal clear coral seas and lush vegetation. Okinawa is the southernmost part of Japan's territory, and Naha International Airport can be reached in two and a half hours by air from Tokyo.

The island chain consists of three major island groups – Okinawa, Miyako and Yaeyama – and about 70 other small islands, some of which are uninhabited.

Okinawa Prefecture measures about 2,388 square kilometres in size, and its population of 1,127,010 (1982 figure) is mainly made up of fishermen and farmers. Its main products are sweet potatoes and sugar cane.

An aerial view of Motobu
Peninsula, the site of the
International Ocean Exposition,
1975.

Crystal-clear coral seas.

History

Okinawa, formally known as Ryukyu, first made its appearance in Japanese written records around the 7th century, but its history in ancient times is not clearly known.

According to tradition, several dynasties succeeded one another there, some of them closely related to ancient Chinese dynasties.

Since the 14th century, the inhabitants of Ryukyu are known to have been actively engaged in trading with neighboring territories including Japan, China, Korea, Java and Sumatra. Ryukyu's close relations with Japan date from 1609, when one of the ruling clans that formed the feudal government, the *Shimazu,* sent a force to occupy Ryukyu with the approval of the central government, and took complete control of the islands.

In modern times, Okinawa was famous as a major battleground during World War II. More than 100,000 Japanese, soldiers and civilians, died in fighting with the American armed forces who landed in April, 1945.

In the post-war period, the United States established powerful military bases on Okinawa, which served as a keystone for its Far Eastern strategy.

Okinawa reverted to Japan in May, 1972, after 27 years of American administration, and became the 43rd prefecture of Japan.

Naha

The largest city of Okinawa, with a population of nearly 302,468, contains the majority of its government buildings, public service facilities, broadcasting stations, newspaper firms, and commercial centers. The visitor's first contact with Okinawa is through Naha International Airport. In and around the city, there still remain a number of landmarks and ruins dating back to the time of the Ryukyu Dynasty.

Southern Battlefields

One hour's drive from Naha will take you to the scenes of the big battles towards the end of World War II.

On the sites there now stand several cemeteries, monuments

172

and towers in memory of the war dead.

Okinawa City

The second largest city of Okinawa, formally known as Koza, is located about 20 kilometres north-east of Naha.

It was transformed from a small village into a modern city with the establishment of large-scale American military bases there after the war.

In a half-hour drive, you can get to the ruins of *Nakagusuku* Castle, the center of the Ryukyu Dynasty. The castle, built some 535 years ago, is one of the architectural wonders of the world. From its walls one commands a fine view of *Nakagusuku* Bay.

Sea Coast State Park

The coastline facing the East China Sea from *Yomitan* Village through *Onna* Village to *Nago* City has been designated as a state park by the Japanese government, for its beautiful panoramic view, characteristic of the sub-tropics.

Along this 40-kilometer stretch of coastline are shallow bathing beaches, sea parks and other tourist attractions.

Iriomote National Park

Iriomote Island is part of the *Yaeyama* island chain lying to the south-west of the main island of Okinawa. It is completely uncultivated and covered with natural jungle. The whole island is an amazing treasurehouse of exotic trees — especially mangrove and palm — and rare animals such as wild boars and wild cats. Sightseeing boats are available for river-trips along the *Urauchi* and *Nakama* Rivers.

Other Tourist Attractions

A bathing-suit is essential on a trip to Okinawa. All over Okinawa there are beaches open to the public all year round. Almost all the beaches are shallow for 200 or 300 metres from the shore and give you a dazzling view of corals and tropical fishes.

Classical court dances of Ryukyu.

A lion dance still performed in Taramashima Island.

Popular Okinawan dances.

Girls putting the finishing touches to bingata dyed fabrics.

Culture, Arts and Public Entertainments

Okinawa has its own culture and customs, distinct from those of the Japanese mainland, as a result of its historical past as an independent dynasty, and its sub-tropical geography.

Okinawan culture, like Japanese, came under strong influences from China, but the process of absorption was different in each case, and gave rise to different cultural forms.

The Okinawan people are very fond of festivals. Each region has its own songs and festivals, and in the towns and villages festivals take place one after another all the year round. Each region has its own music, but uses the same musical instruments — namely the jabisen (a three-stringed instrument covered with snake-skin), the koto (a Japanese harp-like instrument), bamboo flutes, drums and bells.

Classical court dances dating back to the time of the Ryukyu Dynasty are still frequently performed. These dances came originally from China, Japan and some parts of Okinawa, or a combination of these; with the native costumes of the dancers, the bright colors and relaxed atmosphere, they are typical of the southern temperament.

The figures of lions on the rooftops are one of the features of traditional art on Okinawa. Okinawans have long worshipped the lion as the king of all animals. They decorate the roofs of their houses and the entrances to their villages with wooden carved lions in various forms as a charm to drive away evil spirits.

Dyed goods: Making dyed goods, called 'bingata' has been a characteristic art of Okinawa since the 15th century. Natural objects, flowers, animals, birds and other patterns are impregnated on fabrics in various colors by hand.

Textiles: Ryukyu textiles, heavily influenced by Indian and southeast Asian culture, are particularly attractive to female visitors. The geometrical patterns in strong red and blue colors evoke the joys and sorrows of Okinawan women.

Porcelain ware: Ryukyu porcelain, with its 500-year history, is one of the oldest handicrafts in Okinawa. Visitors have an opportunity to see artisans at work in their traditional setting. Other arts and crafts of Okinawa, too, are highly valued among connoisseurs for the beauty of their designs.

Okinawan Food

The hot and humid climate, together with its geographical position, have created a distinctive kind of food in Okinawa. Materials are selected with care to be stored and preserved for a long time. They are treated with oil and garlic like Chinese food.

The typical food of Okinawa is the pig — almost every part of the animal, from head to tail, is used for cooking.

There is a strong local liquor known as 'Awamori', which has been made down the generations for 500 years.

International Ocean Exposition in Okinawa

The first international maritime exposition in world history was held on Okinawa in 1975. The official title of the exposition was "The Internationl Ocean Exposition, Okinawa, Japan, 1975" and its main theme was "The Sea We Would Like To See."

The displays at the various pavilions illustrated the relationship between man and the sea, and how this relationship can be developed in the future. Besides the exhibitions sponsored by foreign governments, there were exhibitions presented by the Japanese government, international organizations and private firms.

The exposition was held on a 1 million square meters (250 acres) site at the tip of the Motobu Peninsula, jutting out westward from the central part of the main island of Okinawa. The area measures 4 kilometers from north to south and 200-400 meters from east to west, and covers both land and sea.

A SHORT VIEW OF LONG HISTORY

Dotaku, copper bell.

1. Prehistoric Ages

The Japanese did not know the art of writing until 552 A. D., when Buddhism and the Buddhist Scriptures written in Chinese characters were introduced into Japan. However, the finds and remains and Chinese records are said to show that a considerably developed group of powers and cultures had already been in existence before 552. This is similar to the case of the civilizations of the Mayas and Aztecs in Yucatan.

The ancestry of the Japanese and the formation of their language are not yet ascertained. Although Japan retains traces of contact with the surrounding nations, such as China, Korea, the Tunguses, the South-East Asia, and the Pacific Islands, it has developed a unique civilization detaching itself from these countries and peoples for a long time. In recent years there is a theory that the powers which succeeded in unifying the nation about the 4th century were the horseriding people who had migrated from Korea to Kyushu and Honshu, but this doesn't go beyond the limits of a theory.

Relics of these prehistoric ages are preserved in the National Museum at Ueno. The old stone implements belonging to the Age of Proto-Jomon were discovered at Iwajuku in Gumma Prefecture, the Jomon earthern-wares in the Tohoku region, notably in Aomori and Akita Prefectures, and the Yayoi wares in the Kansai and the Kyushu and as far north as in the Kanto districts.

Haniwa: Female figure.

Gigaku mask "Goko" (right).

Haniwa and Dogu

What we call *dogu* belongs to the Jomon and Yayoi periods, but specifically it refers to the clay dolls of the former period, which are found in the Tohoku areas. *Haniwa* (clay images) are of the Yayoi period, discovered chiefly in the Kyushu and Kinki districts.

Dogu have complicated and inscrutable figures with linear engravings, whereas the figures of *haniwa* are usually fluent and simple. *Haniwa* have figures of not only men and women, but also houses, ships, horses, dogs and the like. Scholars think that *dogu* were chiefly used for rituals and show traces of woman worship, while that *haniwa* were objects to be buried with dead persons in the tombs for the consolation of their souls.

Ancient fashion of man.

2.   Asuka Period (552~710)

Asuka is an old name of the region within a radius of four miles from Kashihara City near Nara. The Asuka period was the time when, after the state had been unified for the first time in 500 A. D., Japan was beginning to absorb the cultures of China and Korea, which had already possessed highly advanced forms of civilizations. Though the Japanese language belongs to a different language system from that of the Chinese language, Japan, which had so far no means of writing, learned it from the Chinese characters.

This is also the time when Buddhism came into Japan. In this period Japan learned for the first time the Chinese political system in order to strengthen her own, and thereupon were issued the first 'constitution' made up of seventeen articles and the laws concerning the ranks of the court officials. During this period Japan frequently sent parties of students to China.

Reflecting the age of assimilating Chinese culture, the fine arts of Asuka retain vivid cultural influences of China and neighboring, Korea. Besides, since in the civilization of China are lurking those of the ancient Greece, Persia and India, it may be said that Japan has been culturally under the indirect influence of these great ancient countries.

The dawn in Japan of the Chinese or Buddhist arts reaches its height during the years from 645 A. D. to 710 A. D., which are known as the Hakuho period. In the Hakuho period Japan made a further adoption of Buddhist culture, showing at the same time its original cultural development.

Architecture:

Horyuji Temple (Nara Pref.)

Sculpture:

Yakushi Nyorai (*Bhaisajyaguru Vaidurya*) (bronze statue)
......Horyuji Temple (Nara Pref.)

Shaka Sanzon (*Sakyamuni Triad*) (bronze)...Horyuji Temple

Guze Kan-non (*Avalokitesvara*) (wooden) ...Horyuji Temple

Kudara Kan-non (wooden) ....Horyuji Temple

Miroku Bosatsu (*Maitreya*) (wooden)
...... Chuguji Temple (Nara Pref.)
and Koryuji Temple (Kyoto City)

Painting:

Portrait of Lady Maya ......The Tokyo National Museum

Portrait of Komoku-ten (*Virupaksa*) ......Horyuji Temple

Others:

Tamamushi-no Zushi (A miniature Shrine with many golden beetles' alae stuck on) ......Horyuji Temple

Tenju-koku Mandala Shucho (Embroidered Hangings symbolizing Mandala) ......Chuguji Temple (Nara Pref.)

Gigaku-men (A Mask for *Gigaku*)
......The Tokyo National Museum
and Shosoin of Todaiji Temple (Nara City)

Statue of Kan-non (Avaloki-tesvara) (left).

A coin first minted in Japan.

3. Nara Period (710~793)

The Imperial family, did not yet possess absolute power at this period, while the large local families were exercising great influence. Besides, problems concerning the succession of throne rose one after another, and the capital city of Japan was transfered from Otsu near Lake Biwa to Fujiwarakyo in Nara. But, with the removal of the capital to Heijokyo near Nara in 710 A. D., Japan came to have a well-organized, stable form of government. The commerce with China (in the dynasty of Tang) became vigorous again. It is also about this time that the first Japanese chronicles, *Kojiki* and *Nihon-shoki* were written.

Waka, an entirely Japanese form of poetry, flourished about this time, and Japan saw the completion of the *Manyo-shu,* an anthology of 4,500 masterpieces of *Waka.* The culture of this period is called Tempyo Culture.

The characteristics of the fine arts of the Nara period lie in their powerful expression of religious emotions. This is especially true of the statues of Buddha, which look calm and peaceful, yet show realistic and human expressions.

Sculpture:
    Birushana Butsu (Statue of *Buddha Vairocana*)
                  ......Todaiji Temple (Nara City)
    Gakko Bosatsu (Statue of *Candra prabha*) ...Todaiji Temple
    Shitsu Kongoshin (Statue of *Vairadhara*) ...Todaiji Temple
    Kisshoten (Statue of *Mahasri*)   ...Todaiji Temple

Nikko Bosatsu (Statue of *Suryaprabha*)
......Yakushiji Temple (Nara City)
Juichimen Kan-non (Statue of Kan-non or *Avalokitesvara*
with eleven faces carved on the head.)
......Shorinji Temple (Nara Pref.)

Painting:
Kako-Genzai-Inga-Kyo Emaki (Picture Scrolls with Buddhist Scriptures depicting the life of Sakyamuni)
......Daigo-Hoon-in Temple (Kyoto Pref.)
Portrait of Kisshoten (*Mahasri*)
......Yakushiji Temple (Nara City)

Crafts:
An Octagonal Bronze Lantern
......Todaiji Temple (Nara City)
The Sacred Crown of Fukukensaku Kan-non (*Amoghapasa*)
......Todaiji Temple (Nara City)
Shari Reliquary   ......Omi Shrine (Shiga Pref.)

Architecture:
Shosoin Treasure Museum of Todaiji Temple, East Pagoda of Yakushiji Temple, Kon-doh Hall of Toshodaiji Temple Hokke-doh Chapel of Todaiji Temple, Yumedono Chapel in the East Precinct of Horyuji Temple

......(Nara City and Pref.)

4.   Heian Period (794~1184)

A ceremonial robe
of a court lady.

"Armour" laced with red thread.

In the later Nara period, Buddhist priests and the nobility increased their strength and began to fight for the real power. In the end, the Fujiwara family suppressed the others and stood at the helm of the state affairs among the nobles. Japan experienced frequent political disturbances and its society became demoralized, which caused the Imperial capital to be transfered to Heiankyo in Kyoto.

At this time the Japanese found that they had imported enough from China, and so they started to adapt what they had hitherto accumulated in order to develop an original form of culture. They invented *kana* scripts on the model of Chinese characters.

The Heian culture is referred to as 'aristocratic' as it is characterized by gorgeousness. Literature became very popular among court ladies. *A Tale of Genji* and *Makura-no Soshi* are typical of the works produced by those ladies.

But, since the nobles were indulged in amusing themselves in Kyoto and abandoned the management of their fiefs to their retainers or large local families, this brilliant age fell at last into decay.

The Heian period corresponds to the time when Europe witnessed the transitions in art from the later Byzantine to the Romanesque styles. Japan, no longer an imitator of China, began to create its own culture and a brilliant age of fine arts came into being, with a close contact kept with esoteric Buddhism, which was strongly influenced by Brahmanism.

Architecture:

 Enryakuji Temple on Mt. Hiei (Otsu City)
 Kongobuji Temple on Mt. Koya (Wakayama Pref.)
 Kanshinji Temple (Osaka Pref.)
 The Five-Storied Pagoda of Muroji Temple (Nara City)
 Kasuga Shrine (Nara City)
 Kamo Shrine (Kyoto City)
 Ho-o-doh ('Phoenix' Hall) of Byodoin Temple at Uji (Kyoto Pref.)
 Konjiki-doh ('Golden Hall') of Chusonji Temple at Hiraizumi (Iwate Pref.)
 Itsukushima Shrine (Hiroshima Pref.)
 The Five-Storied Pagoda of Daigoji Temple (Kyoto City)

Sculpture:

Taizokai Mandala ......Jingoji Temple (Kyoto Pref.)
Godai Myo-O ......Kyo-O-gokokuji Temple (Kyoto Pref.)
Shitenno (*Lokapala*) ('Four Kings of Heaven')
......Kyo-O-gokokuji Temple (Kyoto Pref.)
Nyoirin Kan-non (Wooden Statue of *Cintamanicakra*)
......Byodoin Temple at Uji (Kyoto Pref.)
Juni Shinsho ('Twelve Warrior-Gods')
......Koryuji Temple (Kyoto Pref.)

Painting:

Junitenzo (an image of cosmos) Saidaiji Temple (Nara City)
Godai Rikkuzo ......Enryakuji Temple (Otsu City)
The Blue Fudo-Myo-O (*Aryacalanatha*)
......Shorin-in Temple (Kyoto Pref.)
Picture Scrolls of *A Tale of Genji* ...... The Masuda family
Picture Scrolls illustrating the founding of Shigisanji Temple
......Shigisanji Temple (Nara Pref.)
Choju Giga ('Sketches of Birds and Beasts') by Bishop Toba
......Kozanji Temple (Kyoto City)

Calligraphers:

Ono-no Michikazu (Tofu) (895~966)
Fujiwara-no Sukemasa (Sari) (943~998)
Fujiwara-no Yukinari (971~1027)

Crafts:

Sawa-Chidori *Makie* (Lacquerware with a picture of Marsh
Plovers) ......Kongobuji Temple (Wakayama Pref.)
Akikusa Cho Cho Kagami (Mirror inlaid with a picture of
Autumn Flowers, Butterflies and Birds)
......The Tokyo National Museum

5. Kamakura Period (1185~1392)

When the Heian period declined, the warriors who governed
the fiefs of the noblemen as their proxies were beginning to gain
power. The Taira family (a *samurai* family) succeeded in putting
down the disputes between the aristocracy and the Imperial
Court and rose to power at Kyoto. But the Emperor and nobles,

Head of "Kongo-Rikishi"
(Vajrapani).

A bonze, *biwa* player.

who were put out from the central power, made a tie with the Minamotos and raised a rebellion to overthrow the Tairas. After this, Yoritomo of the Minamoto family united the country under his rule, with his Shogunate government set up at Kamakura. Though the actual power passed to the Hojos after Yoritomo's death, they held the Shogunate government in Kamakura till 1333. This was the time when the culture of the Kamakura period most flourished and formed the basis of the later Japanese culture.

The culture of the Heian period was aristocratic, but the Kamakura period produced for the first time a simple form of culture called *Buke Bunka* (the culture of the samurai caste). Japan's trade with China, which had been suspended, became vigorous again. It is at this period that Zen Buddhism was first introduced into Japan.

The culture of Kamakura is said to be the culture of architecture and sculpture. The Zen-Buddhist temples erected during the Kamakura period are built after the architectural styles of China in the Sung and Tang dynasties and of ancient India.

The carvings and paintings show a deeper realism. And this was, above all, the age of picture scrolls and landscape paintings (*sansuiga*).

191

Architecture:

The Nandaimon Gate of Todaiji Temple (Nara City)

Shari-den Hall of Enkakuji Temple (Kamakura City)

Kenchoji Temple (Kamakura City)

The Hokuen-doh Chapel of Kofukuji Temple (Nara City)

Sculpture:

Fukukensaku Kan-non ....Todaiji Temple (Nara City)

Miroku Bosatsu (*Maitreya*), by Unkei
......Kofukuji Temple (Nara City)

Sogyo-Hachiman, by Kaikei ......Todaiji Temple

A Statue of Minamoto-no Yoritomo
......The Tokyo National Museum

Painting:

Byobu Folding screens with a Picture of Juniten
......Kyo-O-gokokuji Temple (Kyoto Pref.)

Picture Scrolls illustrating the Miracles of Kasuga Myojin
......Kasuga Shrine (Nara City)

Picture Scrolls illustrating the founding of Kitano Shrine
......Kitano Shrine (Kyoto City)

Picture Scrolls illustrating the Miracles by the Gods at the
Mongol Invasions ......Imperial Property

Calligraphers:

Kujo Yoshitsune of the Gokyogoku School (1196~1206)

Asukai Masatsune (1170~1221)

Munetaka Shinno (Prince Munetaka) (1242~74)

Rankei Doryu (1213~78)

Mugaku Sogen (1226~86)

Muso Soseki (1275~1351)

Crafts:

A *Makie* Hand-Box with a picture of Autumn Landscape
......Izumo Taisha Shrine (Shimane Pref.)

A Large Incense Case with Peony Patterns
......Nanzenji Temple (Kyoto City)

6. Muromachi Period (1392~1572)

In 1274 the Mongols, who had conquered Asia and Eastern Europe, attempted an invasion of Japan, which ended in failure. This was quite lucky for Japan, but the Kamakura Government had already begun to decline and soon fell under the Emperor Godaigo in 1333. But the Emperor was not able to direct the warriors. The Imperial Court disputed over legitimacy within itself, and there were at this period two dynasties in Japan, while local warriors frequently clashed with one another. In this way there were sixty years of continuous wars and revolts until 1392, when Ashikaga Yoshimitsu succeeded in settling the disputes within the Court as well as the civil wars. Yoshimitsu established his Shogunate government at Muromachi in Kyoto, which brought order in the political system. But, like Napoleon's, his sole wish was to become an Emperor himself. He built most luxurious buildings one after another. *Higashiyama Bunka* is the name of the culture he did his best to produce that way in the Muromachi period. His successors followed his example, putting aside the government, which soon caused the local powers to disobey them and the heavy-taxed farmers to rise and riot. It is true, however, that Japan enjoyed the prosperity of commerce and industry, and the development of culture of samurai caste.

In Western Europe the years corresponding to the Muromachi period were the beginning of the Renaissance. Zen Buddhism, introduced in the last period, still penetrated through the intellectual class and became the philosophical foundation of art and politics and learning during this period.

A street of Muromachi period.

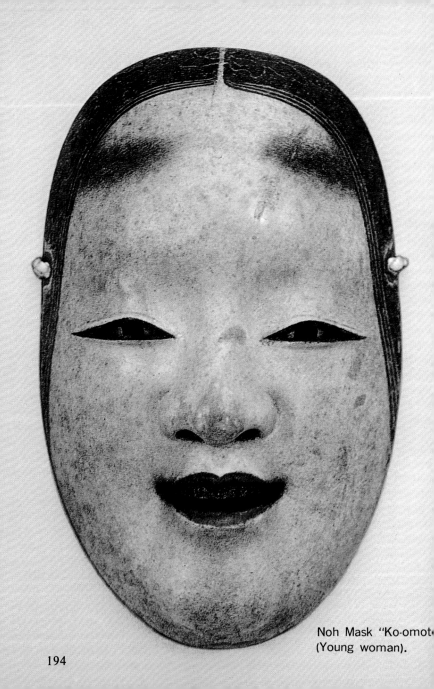

Noh Mask "Ko-omote"
(Young woman).

194

Architecture:
  Kyoto-Gozan (The Five Great Temples at Kyoto):
    Tenryuji, Sokokuji, Kenninji, Tofukuji, and Manjuji.
  Kamakura-Gozan (The Five Great Temples at Kamakura):
    Kenchoji, Enkakuji, Jufukuji, Jochiji, and Jomyoji.
  Others:
    Nanzenji Temple (Kyoto City)
    Daitokuji Temple (Kyoto City)
    Myoshinji Temple (Kyoto City)
  The representative *sho-in** style buildings are:
    Togu-doh of Ginkakuji Temple (Kyoto City)
      * The style of the residence of a samurai family.
Sculpture:
  There are few engravings worth mentioning. Some of the
  above-mentioned temples have masterpiece statues of the
  Buddhist priests who founded them. In addition, there are
  many masterpieces of *Noh* play masks.
Painting:
  The Muromachi period did not produce many masterpieces
  in painting, either, although it had the Tosa School for
  Yamato-e (original Japanese painting represented by Picture Scrolls). Painting in *sumi* ink (*Suiboku-ga*) was brought
  into Japan from China. Many attempts were made in this
  field, and great masters including Sesshu appeared in this
  period. In Yamato-e and landscape painting the following
  are worthy of special note:
  Tsuchigumo-soshi ('Picture Scrolls with a Tale of Ground-
    Spiders') drawn by Tosa Mitsunobu
                    ......The Tokyo National Museum
  Kurama-dera Engi ('Picture Scrolls illustrating the founding
    of Kurama Temple in Kyoto') drawn by Kano Motonobu
                    ......The Tokyo National Museum
  Haboku Sansui drawn by Sesshu
                    ......The Tokyo National Museum
Handicrafts:
  Side by side with the tea ceremony, many masterpieces
  of pottery and *Maki-e* were produced during the Muromachi
  period.

A musket from Portugal.

7. Azuchi-Momoyama Period (1573~1600)

In every district the lords and warriors became powerful by force of arms and strived with one another to gain supremacy. Oda Nobunaga, having built his castle at a convenient place in the north of Aichi Prefecture, overthrew the Muromachi Government in Kyoto. Nobunaga set up his headquarters at Azuchi near Lake Biwa to govern the entire nation. He used muskets introduced from Portugal in 1543. In 1549 Christianity was also brought into Japan. Nobunaga protected it as a means to understand Western civilization.

After he was murdered by one of his supporters, Toyotomi Hideyoshi, who had risen to power by his tactics, took Nobunaga's place. He built a castle at Osaka, a prosperous commercial city, and strived to bring all the country under his sway. He placed a ban on Christianity. Moreover, dreaming of the world conquest, he and his army tried to invade Korea, but his dream was not realized.

Momoyama is a name given in later days to the vicinities of Hideyoshi's Fushimi Castle (Kyoto Pref.).

The buildings that represent this period are castles. Many castles were built in such a way that they might appear beautiful and majestic. In painting, pictures drawn on *fusuma* (sliding room-partitions), characterized by colorful splendor, were very popular. The Higashiyama Culture of the Muromachi period remained alive in the tea ceremony, flower arrangement, landscape gardening and handicrafts during this age, all of which made a marvelous development. Besides, the civilization of Western Europe also flowed into Japan, and Western drawing techniques and typography were introduced.

Architecture:
Himeji Castle (Hyogo Pref.)
Osaka Castle (Osaka City)
Inuyama Castle (Inuyama City, Aichi Pref.)

Nagoya Castle (Nagoya City)

The representative tea-ceremony houses (*cha-shitsu*) are:

Shigure-tei of Kodaiji Temple (Kyoto City)

Jisso-an of Nansoji Temple (Sakai City, Osaka Pref.)

Painting:

Kara-Shishi Byobu (Folding Screens with a Picture of Lions) drawn by Kano Eitoku

"Monkeys on the Bare Trees" drawn by Hasegawa Tohaku

Crafts:

The tea-ceremony encouraged the manufacturing of pottery, and many pieces of local colors were produced during this period. The following are the noted names of the Japanese ceramic products:

Shino, Oribe, Seto, Shigaraki, Iga, Karatsu, Raku.

8. Edo Period (1600~1867)

After Hideyoshi's death, Tokugawa Ieyasu, who had accumulated armed forces in the Kanto district, entered Osaka and overthrew the followers of Hideyoshi. Ieyasu was granted the reigns of the central government by the Imperial Court, and built a great castle (on the site where now the Imperial Palace stands) in Edo (now Tokyo) to establish his Shogunate government. His successors not only managed to put the feudal lords under their direction but also laid down the caste system defining the classes of warriors, farmers, artisans and tradesmen. By so doing, they succeeded in cementing the foundations of the Edo or Tokugawa period. Domestic commerce and industry made a remarkable development, especially in Edo and Osaka. The Edo government had its unstable sides indeed, but on the whole it could maintain order in Japan. Foreign trade was almost prohibited since 1639, but in 1853 Commodore Perry arrived at Uraga, south of Edo, and delivered a letter from President Fillmore, requesting the opening of trade relations. After this, people began to feel they must import the advanced civilization of Europe and America, and started antigovernment movements in every part of the country.

In 1854 the Tokugawa signed a goodwill treaty with the United States, and, within two years, concluded treaties with

A part of the *Makie* reading stand with autumn grasses.

Portrait of a *Kabuki* actor, "Segawa Kikunojo of the third generation", drawn by Toshusai Sharaku (?~1844?).

The procession of *Daimio*.

England, Russia and Holland. These were immediately followed by a commercial treaty with America, which was signed in 1858. But the anti-Bakufu feelings had not subsided until a civil war broke out and in 1867 the last *Shogun* Yoshinobu of the Tokugawa family handed over the central government to the Emperor. Thus the Edo period came to a close and Japan made the first step toward her modernization.

The Tokugawa Bakufu invited scholars, painters, and craftsmen into Edo and made the capital the seat of Japanese culture as well. In the fine arts the painting and handicraft made a great development, while engraving was backward. The architecture represented by dwelling-houses and theaters also made a remarkable progress during this period.

Architecture:
    Nikko Toshogu Shrine (Nikko City)
    The Main Hall of Kiyomizu Temple (Kyoto City)
    The Daibutsuden Hall of Todaiji Temple (Nara City)
    Katsura Imperial Villa (Kyoto City)
    Shugakuin Imperial Villa (Kyoto City)
Artists of Pottery, Gardening and Calligraphy:
    Hon'ami Koetsu   (calligraphy, pottery, lacquer)
    Nonomura Ninsei   (pottery)
    Sano Kenzan   (pottery)
    Sakaida Kakiemon   (pottery)
    Kobori Enshu   (gardening, flower arranging)

Painting:

"Folding Screens with a picture of the Wind-God and the Thunder-God" drawn by Tawaraya Sotatsu

......Kenninji Temple (Kyoto City)

"Folding Screens with a picture of Irises" drawn by Ogata Korin ......Nezu Picture Gallery (Tokyo)

"Folding Screens with a Landscape with a Mansion" drawn by Ike-no Taiga ......The Tokyo National Museum

"Folding Screens with a picture of a Dragon in the Clouds" drawn by Maruyama Okyo

......Kanchi-in Temple (Kyoto City)

Ukiyo-e painters:

Hishikawa Moronobu, Torii Kiyonobu, Utagawa Toyoharu, Kitagawa Utamaro, Toshusai Sharaku, Katsushika Hokusai, Ando Hiroshige.

9. Meiji and Taisho Periods (1867~1926)

In 1868 Edo was renamed Tokyo, and a new era began in the history of Japan. The Meiji government emphasized the development of capitalism and strengthened the military forces in order to develop national power. During this period Japan engaged in two big wars—the Sino-Japanese War of 1894~95 and the Russo-Japanese War of 1904~05. As Japan, a small island-country, won these wars, she suddenly became the focus of the world's attention.

A horse tram-car, train's antecedent.

201

In these years Japan assimilated a great deal of Western civilization and modernized herself to a greater extent. In 1914 Japan took an active part in the First World War.

During the Meiji period the system of education was greatly improved, literature flourished, and modern culture began to be formed. When the War ended, Japan found herself again in an economic depression, where the Showa period started.

Because of the influence of Western civilization, traditional Japanese art became dull for a time. But a revival movement made it possible to produce great masters in the Japanese-style painting.

Japanese-style Painters:
    Hashimoto Gaho   Kano Hogai
    Yokoyama Taikan   Shimomura Kanzan
    Hishida Shunso   Tomioka Tessai
    Hashimoto Kansetsu
Western-style Painters:
    Okada Saburosuke   Yasui Sotaro
    Kuroda Seiki

10. Showa Period (1926~   )

In 1926 Emperor Taisho died and the present Emperor became his successor. The economic inactivity which became apparent during the Taisho years, had at last brought about a financial crisis. And unfortunately enough, Japan had to wage war with her neighbor, China. This was the so-called China Incident of 1937, which led up to an incentive to World War II. In Western Europe the Nazis were extending their power, and Japan joined with Germany and Italy in a greater war.

On Aug. 15, 1945, Japan accepted the terms of Potsdam Proclamation, announcing her unconditional surrender.

Post-war Japan has done her best to be a pacifist nation, and has grown qualified to be a member of the community of nations. In 1956 Japan became a member of the United Nations, and in 1964 the Olympic Games were held in Tokyo. In this way Japan has been completely one constituent of the international

One of domestic rockets, named Lambda.

society and proved worthy of the title of the world's third largest industrial country. When in 1970 the World Exposition was held in Osaka, Japan showed her further development to all the people of the world.

The fine arts of post-war Japan have rapidly followed the artistic movements of the world, but the central figures of the painting circles have been mostly the already eminent artists of pre-war Japan. In quite recent years there is an increasing number of younger artists who take an active part in this field both at home and abroad. The names of representative artists are as follows:

1) Western-style Painters:
   Umehara Ryuzaburo   Fujita Tsuguji
   Sakamoto Hanjiro   Hayashi Takeshi
   Inokuma Gen'ichiro   Oka Shikanosuke
   Wakita Kazu   Ebihara Kinosuke
   Okamoto Taro

2) Japanese-style Painters:
   Fukuda Heihachiro   Maeda Seison
   Okumura Dogyu   Kawabata Ryushi
   Tokuoka Shinsen   Yamaguchi Hoshun
   Domoto Insho   Yasuda Yukihiko
   Kaburagi Kiyokata   Sugiyama Yasushi
   Higashiyama Kaii   Ogura Yuki
   Yamamoto Kyujin   Hashimoto Meiji

3) Wood and Copperplate Printers:
   Munakata Shiko   Hamaguchi Yozo
   Komai Tetsuro   Ikeda Masuo
   Hasegawa Kiyoshi
4) Sculptors:
   Asakura Fumio   Hongo Shin
   Hiragushi Denchu   Sato Gengen
5) Craftsmen:
   Matsuda Gonroku   (gold lacquer)
   Katori Hozuma   (casting)
   Shimizu Nanzan   (chasing, metal-carving)
   Iizuka Rokansai   (bamboo work)
   Itaya Hazan   (ceramics)
   Hamada Shoji   (ceramics)
   Arakawa Toyozo   (ceramics)
   Iwata Toshichi   (glassware)
6) Calligraphers:
   Bundo Shunkai   Suzuki Suiken
   Kawamura Kizan   Matsui Joryu
   Nishikawa Yasushi   Aoyama San-u
   Uno Sesson   Morita Shiryu

JAPAN		B. C.	WORLD
		600000	
			Australopithecus africanus
	Old Stone Age	500000	Pekin Man, Pithecanthropus erectus (Java man).
Proto-Jomon		100000	The Old Man (Neanderthal Man).
		30000	Emergence of the New Man (Cro-Magnon Man).
	Old Stone implements.	8000	
Earliest stage of Jomon	Pit dwellings (several units).		
		3000	Bronze civilization springs up in the Orient.
			Neolithic civilization in the valleys of the Hwang Ho. Bronze in use in India.
Early stage of Jomon	Community of pit dwellings. Flat-bottomed pottery.		The Pyramid Age in Egypt (3000–2500).
		2000	
Middle stage of Jomon	The community spreads to the highlands. Larger clay vessels.		The Chu Dynasty in China.
		1000	
Later stage of Jomon	Numerous kinds of clay vessels. Community with shell-mounds. Kinds of earthenware become regionally different.		Appearance of City-State in Greece Birth of Sakyamuni (565). Birth of Confucius (550). Persian War (492–479).
Last stage of Jomon	Low-land community. Cultivation of rice in Kyushu. The beginning of weaving.	500	
			The Eastern Expedition by Alexander the Great (334–332).
	Jomon earthenware still in use in the north areas of central Japan.	300	
Early stage of Yayoi	Cultivation of rice in west Japan.		Union of China under Shi-Hwang-ti (First Emperor).
	Yayoi earthenware spreads as far as the southern parts of the Tohoku district.	100	
Middle stage of Yayoi	Mirrors and swords made in China used as funeral objects.		
	(There were more than one hundred states in Japan.)	A. D.	Birth of Jesus Christ (4 B. C.).
	Large copper bells (dotaku) appear.		
		100	The Roman Empire at its greates extent (117).
Later stage of Yayoi	Beginning of irrigation. Empress Himiko (d. 248). The earliest tombs. Haniwa (clay images). Worship of gods. Frequent commerce with Korea and China.	300	
	Dispatch of an army to Korea (391).		Great migration of the Germanic race (375).
	Tombs become larger, and ponds and banks built around them.	400	The Roman Empire splits into the Eastern and the Western Empires (395).

Japan		World
Tombs-hills become smaller in scale.		
	500	Fall of the Western Empire of Rome (476).
Numerous *haniwa* images made in the Kanto district.		
		Justinian becomes Emperor of the Eastern Empire of Rome (527).
Introduction of statues of Buddha and Buddhist Scriptures from Korea to the Japanese Court (538 or 552?).		Ascendancy of the Sassanid dynasty in Persia. Birth of Mohammed (570). Age of Seven Kingdoms in England.
Regency of Prince Shotoku (593–622).		Disruption of Frankish Empire.
	600	
Seventeen-article 'Constitution' of Prince Shotoku (604). Horyuji Temple erected (607). Frequent dispatches of students to China.		
		Mohammedan Religion comes into being (629).
Withdrawal of Japanese army from Korea (663). Ranks of officials and Imperial families defined.		
Coins (*Wadokaiho*) minted for the first time.	700	
The shift of the capital to Nara.		The Saracens' conquest of Spain (711).
Completion of *Kojiki*, the first chronicle of ancient Japan (712).		The reign of Emperor Hsuan-tsung in China (712–55).
Completion of *Nihon Shoki* (chronicle) (720).		The Saracens conquer China.
Statue of Buddha of Todaiji Temple completed (752).		
		Baghdad founded (762). Charles the Great ascends the throne (768). Unity of Frankish Empire. The golden age of the civilization of the Saracens.
Founding of Heijo Capital (Kyoto) (794).		
	800	The reconstruction of the Western Empire of Rome (800).
Many temples built by priests returning from China.		Unity of England (828).
		Russia founded (862).
Interruption of dispatches of students to China (894).		
Adjustment of tax system and of fiefs of the aristocracy (902).	900	Fall of the Tang dynasty.
Ascendancy of samurai.		Rollo becomes Duke of Normandy. Otto I founds the Holy Roman Empire (962).
Writing of *Genji Monogatari* (*Tale of Genji*) by Lady Murasaki (1008–20).	1000	
Warriors ravage many places.		The first Crusade (1096~1099).
	1100	
The Tairas suppress the Genji and obtain the central power.		
Taira-no Kiyomori as Prime Minister (1167).		The second Crusade (1147~1149).

Minamoto-no Yoritomo defeats the Taira family and establishes Bakufu at Kamakura (1185).

Notre Dame de Paris erected (1163).
University of Oxford.

The third Crusade (1189~1192).
The fourth Crusade.

1200

Genghis Khan ascends the throne (1202).
Magna Carta signed by the English King John (1215).

Hojo Yasutoki as Shikken (1224–42).

Hanseatic League (1248–54).
Confederation of Rhine (1254).

Unsuccessful Mongol invasion of Japan.

The eighth Crusade (1270).
Kublai Khan founds the Yuan Empire (1271).
Marco Polo arrives in Yuan (1275).
England conquers Wales (1282).
Ottoman Empire founded (1299).

1300

The States-General of France (1303).

The central government in confusion (1334).

The Hundred Years' War (1337–1453).

Ashikaga Takauji assumes the title of Shogun and establishes Bakufu at Muromachi in Kyoto (1338).

Boccaccio writes *The Decameron* (1344–53).
The Black Death in Europe (1348).
University of Vienna founded (1365).
Watt Tyler's Rebellion (1381).
French Civil War (1392).
Li-Ch'eng-kuei founds Korea (1392).

Building of Kinkakuji Temple (Golden Pavilion) by Ashikaga Yoshimitsu (1397).

1400

Noh play flourishes.
Revolts break out in many parts of Japan. Government in confusion.

The civilization of the Maya
Joan of Arc put to death (1431).

Invention of printing by Gutenburg of Mainz (1445).
Bartholomew Diaz discovers the Cape of Good Hope (1486).

Ginkakuji Temple erected (1489).

Christopher Columbus discovers America (1492).

1500

Continuous revolts by Buddhist believers.

Amerigo Vespucci discovers South America.
Peasants War (1524–25).
The heliocentric theory of Copernicus (1530).
End of Inca Empire (1534).

Arrival of Portuguese at Tanegashima and introduction of firearms (1543).
Francis Xavier comes to Kagoshima and introduces Roman-Catholicism (1549).

Fall of Muromachi Bakufu (1574).
Oda Nobunaga sets up Bakufu at Azuchi on Lake Biwa.
Toyotomi Hideyoshi succeeds Nobunaga as Prime Minister (1586).

A ban on Christianity.
Hideyoshi's invasion of Korea (1592).

Tokugawa Ieyasu holds the reins of government.
Completion of Nikko Toshogu Shrine (1617).

The beginning of Kabuki dance.
The ban on Christianity tightened (1638).

Completion of Japan's Isolation policy (1639).

The great fire of the Meireki Era (1657).
Flowering of literature in Edo.

Completion of *Oku-no Hosomichi* (*The Narrow Road of Oku*) by Basho, and his death (1694).

Last eruption of Mt. Fuji (1707).

Great fires continue in Edo.

Peasants' revolts are rampant throughout the country.

Development of medical and scientific studies.

Eruption of Mt. Sakurajima (1779).
Eruption of Mt. Asama (1783).

Freedom of Protestantism accepted in Augsburg (1555).
Wars of Religion in France (1562–98).
Birth of William Shakespeare (1564).
The Netherlands revolt from Spain (1568).

Commencement of the Gregorian Calendar (1582).
The first English migration to North America (1585).

Ascendancy of the Bourbons in France (1589).

1600 England's East India Company (1600).

Galileo Galilei invents telescope (1609).

The Pilgrim Fathers leave England for America.

The Puritan Revolution (1642).

Declaration of the Commonwealth of England (1651).
The Restoration in England (1653).

Isaac Sir Newton discovers the law of gravitation (1687).
The 'Glorious Revolution' in England (1688).

1700

Invention of the steam engine by James Watt (1707).
Reign of the House of Hanover begins in England (1714).

Discovery of the Berling Straits (1728).
Publication of *De l'Esprit des Lois* by Montesquier (1748).

Experiments in electricity by Benjamin Franklin (1752).

Le Contrat Social by Rousseau (1762).
The American War of Independence (1775–83).

The Great French Revolution (1789–94).

208

	1800

Ino Tadataka begins the survey of the whole country (1801).

A decree ordering the expulsion of foreign ships published (1825).
Start of movements for opening the country.

The U. S. envoy, Perry, visits Japan with a message from the American President (1853).
The conclusion of the Japan-U.S. goodwill Treaty (1854).
The conclusion of the Japan-England Treaty and the Japan-Russian Amity Treaty (1854).
The conclusion of commercial treaties with U.S., Holland, Russia, England, and France (1858).

The Edo Bakufu overthrown (1867).

The Ban on Christianity lifted (1876).
Rapid modernization of Japan.
Rapid assimilation of European civilization.
The Sino-Japanese War (1894).

The Russo-Japanese War (1904).

Death of Meiji Emperor and succession of his son Yoshihito (Taisho Emperor) (1912).

Japanese declaration of war on Germany in World War I.

The Great Earthquake in the Kanto District (1923).

Death of Taisho Emperor and accession of Hirohito (Showa Emperor) (1926).

1800

Napoleon's expedition into Egypt (1798).
Napoleon Buonaparte becomes Emperor (1804).
End of the Holy Roman Empire (1806).
America's declaration of the Monroe Doctrine (1823).

The Opium War in China (1840).
The Mexican War (1846–46).

1850

The Communist Manifesto by Karl Marx (1848).

The Crimean War (1854).

Abraham Lincoln becomes President of U.S.A. (1860).
The American Civil War (1861–65).

The opening of the Suez Canal (1869)
A great financial panic in Western Europe and America (1873)

An international peace conference at the Hague (1899).

1900

Theordore Roosevelt becomes American President (1901).

The first stage of the Russian Revolution (1905).

The First World War (1914–18).

The establishment of the Bolshevik government in Russia (1917) The November Revolution).
The Treaty of Versailles signed (1919).
The first meeting of the League of Nations (1920).

The establishment of the Union of Soviet Socialist Republics.

A disarmament conference at Geneva (1927)
Establishment of Hitler's cabinet in

209

Japan quits the League of Nations (1933)

The formation of the Tripartite Alliance of Japan, Germany and Italy (1940).

Japan declares war on the United States and her allies (1941).

Acceptance of the terms of Potsdam Proclamation (1945).

Germany (1932).

The Second World War (1939–45).

The Yalta Conference (1945).

Formation of the United Nations Organization (1945).

Formation of the United Nations Educational, Scientific, and Cultural Organization (UNESCO) (1946).

The International Declaration of Human Rights (1946).

The North Atlantic Treaty (1949).

1950

Signing of the Peace Treaty with U.S. at San Francisco (1951).

Start of NHK television broadcasts (1953).

The Korean War (1950).

Earth satellites launched by Russia (1957) and by U.S. (1958).

John F. Kennedy becomes U.S. President (Aug. 1960).

Assassination of President Kennedy (Nov. 1963).

The Olympic Games convene in Tokyo. (Oct. 1964).

Opening of World EXPO'70 in Osaka (Mar.1970)

Apollo XI launched by the United States. succeed in landing on the moon (July 1969).

Winter Season Olympic Games convene in Sapporo (Feb. 1972).

Agreement of Peace in Vietnam at Paris (June 1973).

Completion of the Guest House at Akasaka (May 1974).

Saigon Falls (Apr. 1975)

Opening of International Ocean Exposition in Okinawa (July 1975)

The ceremony in commemoration of the Emperor's 50 years of reign (Nov. 1976).

The 21st Olympics (Montreal, July 1976).

Death of Mao Tse-tung (Sept. 1976).

New Tokyo International Airport (Narita) opened (May 1978).

Tokyo Summit held (June 1979).

1980

The 22nd Olympics (Moscow, July 1980).

Portpia 81 opened (Kobe City, March 1981).

Iran-Iraq war (Sept. 1980).

Forkland Strife (Apr. 1982).

Tohoku, Joetsu New Trunk Lines (JNR) opened (1982).

THE ECONOMY AND INDUSTRY OF JAPAN

A country with a small area and a dense population would have nothing to depend upon but its industrial power in order to rank with the nations of the world. It is the same with Japan. It is only through her industrial capacity that Japan has been able to make unparalleled rapid development since the end of World War II.

Agriculture

Because about 70% of the total Japanese land area is covered by forest, only 15% or 5,540,000 hectares is suitable for cultivation. On this small area, about 7% of the total workforce was engaged in agriculture in 1981. The number of agricultural labourers per 1 hectare of cultivated land is 1.3 persons in Japan. Comparing this with other developed countries, the ratios are as follows: 0.1 person in England, 0.2 person in France, 0.3 person in West Germany and 0.02 person in U.S.A. As noted the farming population per 1 ha of arable land in Japan is extremely high compared with these countries. This situation is ascribable to the fact that the labour intensive rice crop still plays a major part in Japanese agriculture. The arable land in Japan is utilized in the following manner: 57% as paddy fields, 23% as dry fields for vegetables, beans and other grains and the rest as orchards and stock-farms.

The farming population has remarkably decreased during the high economic growth period in the '60s and '70s. This was due to the increasing demand for manpower with the growth of manufacturing industries which resulted in a major movement of farmers to the factories to fill up the labour shortage.

The conspicuous shift of the agricultural population to other industries was particularly prevalent for small land holders and the younger generation. According to an Agricultural Census, the number of farming households consistently decreased from some 4,950,000 in 1975 to 4,560,000 in January 1982. Out of that total about 600,000 households were full-time and the rest part-time. As of 1981, the farming population stood at 21,080,000, 16% of which were over 65 years old. One of the largest agriculture problems in Japan is the aging of the workforce. But, on the other hand,

213

that increase is accelerating the mechanization of Japan's agriculture. According to a survey conducted by the Ministry of International Trade and Industry, as of May 1980, there were 2,750,000 tillers, 1,470,000 wheeled tractors, 1,750,000 rice transplanters, and 1,620,000 binders.

The agriculture sector is also under pressure to liberalize agriculture trade. The U.S.A., Canada, Australia, New Zealand, China, Taiwan, Brazil, et. al. are all urging that the barriers to agriculture products be liberalized. For many of these countries, Japan represents a key export market. The value of foodstuff imports steadily increased from $14,400 million in 1979 to $16,800 million in 1982. For various reasons, the Japanese government must continue to expand imports of agricultural products, such as lemons and bananas. From now on, agriculturists, such as onion growers, will have to be more competitive with foreign farmers, such as those in New Zealand, concerning prices.

Forestry

There were approx. 25,285,000 ha., of woodland in Japan per a recent survey. This corresponded to 70% of the total land area. Japan consumes about 100 million cubic feet of wood annually. 60% of forests are privately owned, and the rest by state and local entities.

Forestry management is also under modernization, but the demand for pulp and building wood is increasing. Consequently, Japan imports a great quantity of lumber from Alaska, U.S.S.R., and Canada, but still it does not come up to even one-third of the demand.

Fisheries

Japan's fisheries production increased a little from 10,750,000 tons in 1977 to 11,320,000 tons in 1981. However, the number of people engaged in fishing continued to show a gradual decrease from 379,000 in 1977 to 367,000 in 1981. Since the 200 sea-mile zone was established, Japan's fisheries industry has begun to change from 'fishing by catching' to 'fishing depending upon imports'. The value of imports of marine products in 1980 totaled 764,300 million yen.

214

Underground Resources

Not blessed with mineral resources, Japan has to import most of them from abroad. In 1981, for example, $3,504 million of iron ore was imported. This means that Japan depends almost entirely on imports for iron ore.

The consumption of petroleum shows a yearly increase in Japan, and in 1979 it amounted to 4,535,000 barrels. It is estimated that by 1986, consumption of fuel oil will reach 204,072,000 kl, and that of heavy oil, 83,399,000 kl.

When an oil crisis occurred in 1972, oil problems in Japan entered a new phase. In near future, more severe competitions to secure petroleum resources in the world will be unavoidable.

Little petroleum is produced in Japan. Akita and Niigata prefectures have some oil fields indeed, but the output reaches only 1 per cent of the total demand.

Japan is comparatively rich in natural gas, and had a yearly output of 2,787 million m^3 in 1978, which is used as one of the resources for the chemical industry as well as fuel.

The amount of coal deposits in Japan is estimated at about 20,000 million tons. Japan is rich in coal, but the output of coal has shown a decrease since petroleum took its place as the principal fuel. In 1978 the output of coal was only 19 million tons. Japan is dependent upon import for ores, such as copper, aluminum and uranium.

Trade

After the liberalization of foreign trade in April, 1964, Japanese enterprises have been remarkably modernized in structure and greatly enlarged in scale. In 1981 the total export of Japan amounted to 152,030 million dollars, and the chief export commodities were automobiles, electrical/electronic machinery, precision instruments, and heavy chemical products, with the United States standing first among the export countries, followed by the U.S.S.R., Saudi Arabia and South Korea.

216

The Atomic Power Laboratory, in Ibaraki Pref.

The invisible trade, including shipping and the like, and the capital accounts have always been in the black. In 1981, the figure of export showed $152,030 million, import $143,290 million, and the trade balance went into the black of $20,358 million.

Electric Power

With many rivers of rapid current, Japan had greatly relied upon the hydro-electric process for the output of electric power, but in recent years the thermal process has made great progress. In 1981 the output of thermal power reached 70 per cent of the national total of 583,245 million KWh. The government is planning to expand the power generation equipment in order to increase the total output of electric power.

In Japan the processes of atomic power generation have been pursued as one of the projects of the peaceful development of atomic power. In 1964 Japan imported a power reactor of the improved Calder-Hall type, which is being tested at Tokaimura, Ibaraki Pref. The tested reactor is capable of generating 160,000 KW of electric power. In addition to this imported reactor, twenty-one national atomic power stations are expected to be constructed in Japan by 1985, with an estimated output of 60,000,000 KW of electricity.

Manufacturing Industry

This industry can be divided into the material and processing/engineering industry. The oil crisis triggered by the Mid-East war in the fall of 1973 has greatly changed this industry. At the present, the business climate is completely different from that of 10 years ago.

During the 1970 − 1981 period, Japanese exports increased from $19,318 million to $152,030 million. In 1970, the material industry was about 35% or over one-third of total exports. But in 1981, the share dropped to 21.1% while the processing & engineering industry grew from 46% to 65.8% or two-third of total exports.

Why has this violent change occurred? It's due in large part to the inability of the material industry to cope with the sharp oil price hikes since 1973. Many material industries are depressed − petrochemicals, chemical fertilizers, aluminum smelting and cement, to mention only a few. Until recently, all these had been highly competitive internationally.

218

In contrast to the above, manufactured goods not affected much by the soaring oil prices have grown into front runners all over the world — watches, facsimiles, VTRs, automobiles, robots, copiers, and cameras, to mention only those leading the peek.

These tendencies are expected to continue for the time being.

Various manufacturing industries in Japan are compared in the following tables.

A sparkling bucket. Hirohata factory (in Himeji City) of Nippon Steel Corporation

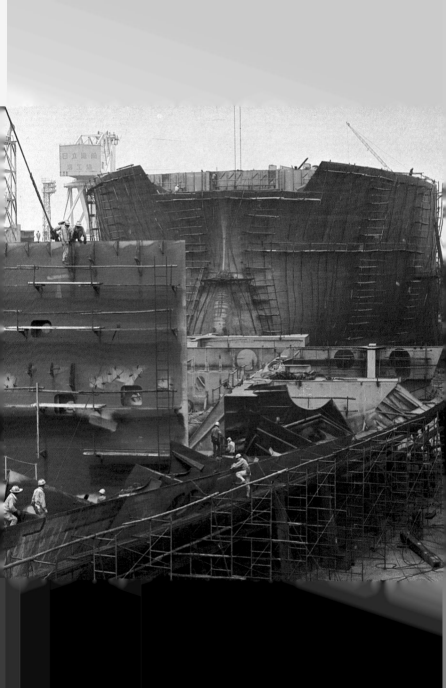

Merchant Vessels

(Tonnage Launched) in 1980

Japan	7,288	(1,000 tons)
Korea, Republic of	629	
Brazil	615	
U.S.A.	558	
Spain	509	

(Source: U.N. "Statistical Year Book)

Automobile Production in 1978

U.S.A.	12,458	(1,000 units)
Japan	9,269.2	
West Germany	4,218	
France	4,075.3	
U.S.S.R.	2,074	
Italy	1,656.6	

(Source: U.N. "Statistical Year Book)

Petroleum Consumption in 1978

U.S.A.	6,879,017	(1,000 barrels)
Japan	1,876,767	
West Germany	1,112,647	
France	791,692	
England	695,152	

(Source: I.P.A.)

Machinery Exports in 1978

West Germany	70,117	(1,000,000 dollars)
U.S.A.	62,540	
Japan	61,921	
France	28,788	
England	28,064	

(Source: OECD)

Whaling in 1978–1979

U.S.S.R.	6,261	(units)
Japan	1,867	
Peru	·1,042	
Spain	547	
Iceland	440	

(Source: U.N. "Statistical Year Book)

Plastics Production in 1977

U.S.A.	11,715	(1,000 tons)
Japan	5,164	
U.S.S.R.	3,300	
West Germany	3,245	
France	2,140	

(Source: U.N. "Statistical Year Book")

Sulfuric Acid Production in 1978

U.S.A.	34,854	(1,000 metric tons)
U.S.S.R.	22,411	
Japan	6,437	
West Germany	4,671	
France	4,587	

(Source: U.N. "Statistical Year Book)

Synthetic Fiber Production in 1979

U.S.A.	3,484	(1,000 tons)
Japan	1,363	
West Germany	760	
Taiwan	521	
South Korea	477	
England	381	

(Source: Japan Chemical Fibers Association
"World Man-made Fiber Research")

Paper Production in 1979

U.S.A.	57,567	(1,000 metric tons)
Japan	17,861	
Canada	13,789	
U.S.S.R.	9,236	
West Germany	7,444	

(Source: U.N. "Statistical Year Book)

Cement Production in 1978

U.S.S.R.	126,959	(1,000 metric tons)
Japan	84,882	
U.S.A.	77,548	
Italy	38,232	
West Germany	33,959	

(Source: U.N. "Statistical Year Book)

Nitrogenous Fertilizer Production in 1977

U.S.A.	9,939	(1,000 tons)
U.S.S.R.	9,025	
France	1,470	
Japan	1,446	
West Germany	1,305	

(Source: U.N. "Statistical Year Book
Note: Figures exclude industrial)

TV Sets Production in 1978

Japan	13,927	(1,000 sets)
U.S.A.	9,309	
West Germany	4,239	
England	2,417	

(Source: U.N. "Statistical Year Book)

Exports, f.o.b. in 1980

U.S.A.	216,668	(1,000,000 dollars)
West Germany	192,930	
Japan	129,248	
England	115,350	
France	111,251	

(Source: U.N. "Statistical Year Book)

Production of Electricity in 1980

U.S.A.	2,356,139	(1,000,000 kWh)
U.S.S.R.	1,295,000	
Japan	612,040	
West Germany	368,772	
Canada	366,677	

(Source: U.N. "Statistical Year Book
1979–1980")

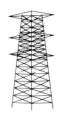

Newspapers Circulation in 1977

U.S.S.R.	102,462	thousands
Japan	62,221	
U.S.A.	62,159	
West Germany	25,968	
England	22,900	

(Source: U.N. "Statistical Year Book)

Pipelines of petroleum refining plant. Sumitomo Chemical Company.

·The belt-production of video tape recorders.

Morning rush hour.

NEW JAPAN

Some foreigners who visit Japan to get in touch with the mysteries of the Orient for the first time might feel their visit hopeless immediately after they have landed at Tokyo International Airport. The modern-style buildings standing close together, the three-dimensional expressways, and floods of motorcars . . .

Japan is now the third largest industrial country of the world. After the war Japan has risen from the ruins and ashes left in the wake of her defeat, and has done all she could to recover the economy and to develop commerce and industry.

A little smaller than the state of California, Japan is inhabited by some 117 million people. In a single year the Japanese produce 15,174,000 cameras, 156,341,000 watches, 4,759,000 electric washing machines, 360,338 pianos, read 54,712,000 newspapers. In a single year 53,634,000 telephones and 106,344 (sets) electronic computers are fully used, 30,031,000 television sets, and 2,190,000 students attend 980 colleges.

However, the Japanese are born to have a high regard for their traditions, and have carefully preserved the cultural assets of the past, which are at present well harmonized with the new. It is the same with the food, clothing and housing of the Japanese. Every day we repeat a "return to Japan", the desire to feel at home among things genuinely Japanese. What might have been born thousands of years ago in Japan is often deeply implanted today in our dishes on the table, in our everyday clothes, in the styles of our houses, and in our furniture.

Formal Japanese dishes.

The correct way to hold the chopsticks.

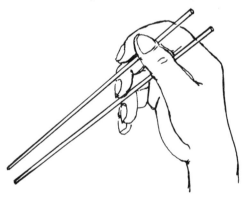

EVERYDAY LIFE

Food

As is also the case with the countries of South-East Asia, the principal food in Japan is rice. It is supposed that rice was first introduced from South-East Asia before the Christian era. Today, the cultivation methods have so developed that rice and wheat are generally cultivated alternately, so that excellent wheat has also come out, while the techniques of bread making have made rapid progress. But, we are still living on rice, since it is not easy for us to change our taste, which has been cherished for the past two thousand five hundred years.

In the days of antiquity, when Buddhism had not yet been introduced, the Japanese seem to have been eating wild animals. But after the 6th century they took the teachings of Buddhism to heart and stopped eating beasts, which are rich in albuminous substances. Instead, they began to catch and eat fish as the source of protein.

In the 19th century Japan's isolation was finally broken and European civilization flowed into the country. After that the Japanese came to eat a lot of animal food as they do now. But, as Japan is blessed with the sea, fishing products still serve as our important source of animal protein.

In preparing rice we boil it thoroughly in an adequate quantity of water until it becomes tender with little water left in it. As an indispensable side dish, we have a kind of soup called *Misoshiru*. *Miso* is made from soy beans or wheat grains which, after steamed, is fermented and kept with salt for about half a month. It is nutritious and is a very important condiment together with soy sauce.

We also have some pickles made by preserving cucumbers and other vegetables in salt rice-bran paste.

These foods appear on the table every day. In addition, there are *tempura* (seafood or vegetable fritters), *tofu* (bean-curds), *sashimi* (raw seafoods), and *nori* (laver).

Japanese Dishes Popular among Foreign Visitors

Sukiyaki

This is a food you cook on a table and serve yourself. A foreigner need not worry about it in a restaurant because a waitress will tell him how to cook it. Slices of beef and vegetables, such as stone-leeks, slices of Chinese cabbage, mushrooms and bean-curd squares, are cooked in a shallow iron saucepan. The beef is preferably tendonless, lean, tender, evenly and mottled with fat. Incidentally, there are cows which are specially raised for the *sukiyaki* beef. These cows are given beer and *sake* as well as ordinary feeds, and are massaged daily. (The cities of Matsusaka and Kobe are noted for such cows.)

Nabe-mono

The *nabe* dish is similar to *sukiyaki,* but there are various kinds of it, such as *tori-nabe* (chicken), *yose-nabe* ('chowder'), *mizutaki* ('chicken boiled plain'), *fugu-chiri* (swellfish), *anko-nabe* (angler), etc. Of course, all of them are done with vegetables. In cooking, you use a vessel made of clay and a bit deeper than that for *sukiyaki.* Like *sukiyaki,* the *nabe*-foods lose much of their flavor if they are over cooked. In eating, you dip them in a soup flavored with lemons or oranges. When you have tried any of them once, why don't you venture to cook them according to your own taste?

Soba

Soba is a kind of paste, prepared from buckwheat flour, in the form of spaghetti pieces. In cooking, we generally use the *soba* sticks which are dried up and are commonly sold in shops.

The Japanese are so fond of *soba* dishes that you can find *soba* shops even in the remotest places of Japan. In cooking the secret lies in the boiling of *soba* and the making of good soup, and every shop has its own 'hereditary' way of making it.

Tempura

Tempura are fish, shrimp, or vegetables coated with a batter of wheat flour and boiled up in vegetable salad oil (made from

230

rape-seeds, soy beans, or sesame seeds). In eating you dip them in a specially prepared soup. Every *tempura* restaurant has a proprietary technique of preparing this kind of soup.

Clothing

Today the Japanese usually wear Western clothes. The traditional Japanese clothes are called *kimono*. The *Kimono* is beautiful and also suitable to be worn at home. But, since it is not convenient for movement, it is becoming less popular as our life becomes more modernized. We do not wear it every day, except some who are, like artists and geisha girls, engaged in special occupations. *Kimonos* are chiefly worn on holidays, at wedding ceremonies, funerals, and at parties. They are also worn for formal visits and meetings, and sometimes on special occasions for foreign tourists.

As for aged people in Japan, the majority of them wear *Kimonos* every day, and in most cases have a few of them, whether men or women. *Haori,* a kind of cloak worn over the *Kimono* proper on ceremonial occasions, has family crests dyed on its sleeve, breast and back. A kind of short coat called *happi* was a working habit worn by lumber dealers and carpenters.

Japanese women in *Kimonos* may probably be all that has so far been introduced abroad about *Kimono*, but men also wear them at home since they think them convenient and elegant that way. *Kimono* means nothing but clothes. The origin of *Kimono* dates back to the 8th century A. D. It developed little by little after it first appeared, and in the 14th century the distinction became clearer between the kinds of *Kimono* for men and those for women. It was originally the clothes in which people relaxed at home, but as outdoor clothes, men usually wear with a *hakama* on it, in the style of a two-piece dress. Kinds of *Kimono* range from an underwear to a coat-like upper garment, and of course we adjust the thickness and quality of the materials to the changes of the seasons. The *Kimono* beautifully woven, dyed and embroidered shows the superior techniques of weaving, dyeing and embroidering in our country. *Obi, tabi, geta* and *zori* are indispensable accessories to the *Kimono*.

In visiting-kimono.

A 'Sumo' wristling scene.

Ocha-no-ma, The Livingroom

Ocha-no-ma is a room where a family gets together for tea, and is commonly used as a dining room as well. Today 91.7 per cent of the families in Japan have TV sets, so their domestic pastimes mostly center around them.

Tatami

Just as the Japanese cannot give up rice and *miso*-soup, so in the case of furniture they cannot part with *tatami*. *Tatami* is a kind of mat, 5.6 feet long, 3 feet broad and 4 inches thick, made of rushes which are dried and plaited together. The size of a room is usually indicated by the number of *tatami*.

In big cities like Tokyo, modern apartment houses are on the increase, but their rooms are as a rule still matted with *tatami*. It is the same with most Japanese inns, except Western style Hotels. As the *tatami* mats are always kept clean, you are supposed to take off your shoes. Foreign tourists in Japan should remember this when they visit Japanese families.

Young salaried man and his wife enjoy a TV program in their *ocha-no ma*, the living room.

SPORTS

Japanese Arts of Self-Defense

Traditional Japanese fighting arts, which are classified into *kendo, judo, karate* and more than twenty-seven other kinds, made remarkable progress in the 15th century. They made further progress when master hands appeared and taught them to warriors. Today, *kendo* and *judo* are included in the practical lessons in physical education at schools, either as sports or as arts of self-defense. *Judo* is already internationally very popular, and was formally adopted in the Olympic Games for the first time in 1964.

Sumo

Sumo is one of the national sports of Japan, and has now a considerable number of fans. *Sumo* matches are played within the straw bales of a ring, 15 feet in diameter, built on hardened sand. In *sumo* there are no restrictions on the weight of the players as in boxing and wrestling. In an actual bout, the player forcing the other out of the ring, or making any part of his body except the soles of his feet touch the ground, wins.

In the senior division (Maku-uchi) there are 5 ranks, of which the highest is called Yokozuna. A series of 15-day tournaments is held six times a year. One player has one match a day, and the winner is decided from the highest number matches won.

Modern Sports

Japan has imported many new sports from foreign countries since 1868, the year of the dawn of modern Japan. The athletic games which are played in Japan outnumber those of the Olympics. Comparatively small in stature, the Japanese have shown remarkable results in gymnastics, wrestling, volleyball, long-distance races, and so forth. As for the sports the Japanese enjoy watching, there is the professional baseball, but in a few years soccer and Rugby football are expected to win great popularity with the Japanese.

A *kendo* match at the national student championship (right).
Buttock. A practice at the Kodokan, *Judo* gymnasium (below).

A Japanese woman swimmer.

THE POLITICAL SYSTEM

Japan is a nation with the Emperor as its symbol and the sovereignty resting with the people. With the end of World War II, the old constitution was revised, and the new constitution of Japan, embodying principles for the government, was proclaimed on Nov. 3, 1946. The new constitution asserts that the sovereign power resides with the people, denying the privileges regarding social status, family origin, sex, and so forth. The National Diet operates as the sole law-making organ of the State. The outline of political system of Japan is shown in the following diagram:

OUTLINE OF THE JAPANESE GOVERNMENT

NATIONAL DIET

House of Representatives
  (511 members)
House of Councillors
  (252 members)
Secretariat
Legislative Bureau
Standing Committees
Special Committees
  Secretariat
  Legislative Bureau
  Standing Committees
National Diet Library
Impeachment Court

SUPREME COURT

High Courts
District Courts
Summary Courts
Family Courts

CABINET

Board of Audit
National Personnel Authority
Prime Minister's Office
Ministries and Agencies.
  Justice
  Foreign Affairs
  Finance
  Education, Science and Culture
  Health and Welfare
  Agriculture, Forestry and Fishery
  Transportation
  Postal Services
  Labor
  Construction
  International Trade and Industry
  Home Affairs
  Defence
  Economic Planning
  Scince and Technology
  Environment National Land
  Imperial Household
  Police

EDUCATION

The percentage of the people of lower ages in Japan who receive compulsory education is the highest in the world. Here, Japan is the most modern of all the nations of the world. The

237

The National Diet Building.

statistics show that the percentage of the children enrolled in elementary and junior high schools was 100.0% in 1970.

Children receive 9 years of compulsory education, entering elementary schools at 6 and finishing junior high at 15. The length of the course is shorter than in England, where it is 10 years, but stands comparison with that of the United States or Germany.

There are also 3 years of senior high school, 4 years of college, and 5 years of graduate school (including the doctrate course). The following table gives information about other kinds of schools.

		Schools	Teachers & Profs.	Pupils & Students
Compulsory				
Primary	(6 years)	25,043	475,037	11,901,526
Junior high	(3 years)	10,879	269,641	5,623,978
Uncompulsory				
High		5,213	248,103	4,457,045
University & College		455	107,422	1,817,649
Junior College		526	16,866	374,273
Preschool for Infant		15,152	99,587	2,227,550
Other (for blind, deaf and dumb, weak children)		882	36,367	94,864

While school education has been popularized in this way, social education has not quite spread in Japan. This is chiefly because a great many people leave villages and flow into cities as the difference in living standards between them has grown larger and also because the education policies for the general public have not been quite satisfactory, to say nothing of the educational facilities for them. However, thanks to the spread of school education, there is nobody in Japan today, except the physically and mentally handicapped, that cannot write and read.

Statistics show that in 1960 the percentage of illiteracy in Japan was 2.2% of the total population, which is also the case in the United States. Of course, Japan has the smallest percentage in Asia.

It is interesting that in Japan the figure is 1.0% in the case of men and 3.3% in that of women, while in America it is men's 2.5% against women's 1.8%.

A kindergarden.

INDEX

Agriculture 213
Aizuwakamatsu 30
Akan, Lake 20
Akikusa Cho Cho Kagami 189
Akka-do Cave 29
Ama 111
Aoi, Festival 117
Aoyama San-u 204
Arakawa Toyozo 204
Art of self-defence 234
Asahi, Mt. 20
Asahi Newspaper 68
Asakura Fumio 204
Asakusa 53
Asama, Mt. 38
Ashi, Lake 87
Ashikaga Yoshimitsu 193
Aso, Mt. 164
Asuka Period........................182
Asukai Masatsune 193
Atami 87
Atom-bomb 162, 167
Atom-bombed Dome..............161
Atomic Power Laboratory 117
Awa Folk Dance.....................159
Azekura-zukuri 63
Azuchi-Momoyama Period.......196
Bakufu 25, 48, 85
(cf. Shogunate Government)
Bandai Asahi 30
Basho 33
Bed-town 45
Birushana Butsu 185
Biwa, Lake 119, 132
Blue Fudo-Myo-O 189
Bodhidharma 134
Bon Odori (Festival Dance) 81, 147
Bridgestone Gallery 71
Buddhism 78, 112, 138, 175
Buddhist Culture 175
Budo-kan Hall 52, 63

Bugaku 146
Buke Bunka 191
Bundo Shunkai 204
Bunraku 147
Beppu 163
Buson 33

Calligraphy 102, 134
Central Post Office 48
Ceramic, Names of 197
Chikamatsu Monzaemon..........147
Chinese Art,
    Character 103, 182, 183, 188
Chishima Current 92
Choju Giga 189
Chugoku District 114
Chukyo Industrial Zone 218
Chusonji Temple 29
Chuzenji, Lake 37
Clark, Dr. 17
Climate 8, 21
Clothing 10, 231
Communications Museum..........71
Coronation Ceremony 131

Daibutsu 139
Daibutsu-den Hall 139, 200
Daibutsu of Kamakura 87
Daigoji Samboin Temple..........127
Daimio 48
Daisetsu, Mt. 20
Daisetsu Suzuki 134
Daitokuji Temple 195
Dammari 58
Danchi 45, 242
Dengaku 146
Department Store 73
Dewa mountains..................25, 30
Dogu 174
Domoto Insho 203
Dried-up Landscape
    Gardens 122
Dwelling 8

(Left) "Danchi", a mass of standardized apartments, is a town itself including many shops, banks, theaters, schools and parks. One hundred and fifty thousand people live in 30 thousand homes in Senri Newtown, Osaka.

Earthquake 76, 92
Ebihara Kinosuke 203
Edo, period &
    place 76, 103, 147, 197
—, Castle 46, 196
Education 237
Electric Power......................218
Enkakuji Temple 80
Enoshima Island 85
Eri 133

Fenollosa 141
Firework 10, 12, 22
Fisheries 214
Five Bridges of Amakusa 167
Five-Storied Pagoda 141, 188
Flower Arrangement 99
Food 10, 229
Forestry 214
Fude 103
Fujiwara Clan..................... 29, 40
Fujiwara-no Sukemasa............189
Fujiwara-no Yukinari 189
Fujita Tsuguji 203
Fukukensaku Kan-non 192
Furin 11
Furyu-no-michi 99
Fushimi Inari Shrine 131

Gagaku.................................146
Gakko-Bosatsu 185
Gardening 8
Genji, A tale of 188
—, picture scroll of 189
Gigaku 146
Ginkakuji Temple...................195
Ginza...........................52, 54, 74
Gion 117, 132
Godai Hall 29
Godai Myo-o......................189
Godai Rikkuzo 189
Goju-no Toh 142
Goshiki-numa 30
Gosho 131
Great South Entrance 139
Guze Kan-non 183
Gyoki 136

Haboku Sansui 195
Hachimantai 28
Hachirogata..........................30
Haiku 33
Hakone 87
Hakuho Period 183
Hamada Shoji 204

Hamaguchi Yozo 204
Hamamatsu 107
Hanetsuki 79
Haniwa 182
Hanshin Industrial Zone 218
Happi 231
Hasegawa Kiyoshi 204
Hashimoto Gaho 202
Hashimoto Kansetsu 202
Hashimoto Meiji 203
Hato Bus 46
Hayashi Takeshi 203
Heian, Period & Culture 186
Heian Shrine 122
Hibiya Park 48
Higashiyama Culture 196
Himeji 159
Himeji, Castle 158, 196
Hina, doll 80
Hina Matsuri 79
Hiragushi Denchu 204
Hiroshima 162
Hishida Shunso 202
Hishikawa Moronobu 201
Hitachi 39
Hokuen-doh Chapel 192
Hokuriku 24
Hon'ami Koetsu 200
Honganji Temples..................127
Honshu 3, 92
Ho-o-doh 188
Horyuji Temple 138, 141, 183
Hot spring 20, 38, 87

Iizuka Rokansai 204
Ikebukuro 53
Ikeda Masuo 204
Imperial Court 85, 139
Imperial Palace 46, 76
Imperial Theater 48, 59
Inari 131
Inawashiro, Lake 30
Inazo Nitobe 17
Inokuma Gen'ichiro 203
Iron Consumption 3
Ise 110
Ishiyama Temple 151
Isolation 164
Itako, medium......................28
Itaya Hazan 204
Itsukushima Shrine 188
Iwata Toshichi 204
Izumo Taisha Shrine 114

244

Japan Alps.........................95, 107
Japan Inland Sea 11, 157
Japan Folkcraft Museum 70
Japan Sea ....24 (cf. 92)
Jidai Festival 117
Jodo Shin Sect 127
Judo gymnasium 235
Jufukuji Temple 195
Juichimen Kan-non 186
Juni-Shinsho 189
Juniten 192
Junitenzo 189

Kabuki-za, Theater 58, 146, 147
Kaburagi Kiyokata 203
Kaidan-in Hall 139
Kagura 146
Kakejiku 101
Kako-Genzai-Inga-Kyo Emaki...186
Kamakura 85
Kamakura, made of snow 25
Kamakura Period 81
Kanazawa 114
Kamo Shrine 188
Kano Hogai 204
Kanzo Uchimura 17
Kara Dera 167
Kara-Shishi Byobu.................197
Karate 234
Karesansui Teien 122
Katori Hozuma 204
Katsura Imperial Villa 9, 127
Katsushika Hokusai............91, 201
Kawabata Ryushi 203
Kawamura Kizan 204
Kaza-hana 25
Kenchoji Temple 195
Kendo 234
Keihin Industrial Zone 218
Kenroku Park 114
Kenzo Tange 65
Kii Peninsula 110
Kimono 10, 231
Kisshoten 185, 186
Kitagawa Utamaro 201
Kitakami mountains 25, 29
Kita-kyushu City 170
Kiyomizu Temple 119, 122
Kobori Enshu 200
Kokichi Mikimoto 111
Kokusai Theater 59
Komazawa Physical
  Olympic Park 62
Komai Tetsuro 204
Kombinat 110

Kondo Hall of Horyuji
  Temple 141, 142
Kondo Hall of Toshodaiji
  Temple 186
Konjiki-doh 29, 188
Kojiki 185
Kuju, Mt. 164
Kurashiki 159
Kuroda Seiki 202
Kusasenri 165
Kyogen 146
Kyoto International
  Conference Hall 125

Maeda Seison 203
Magosaburo Ohara 159
Maiko 132
Main Island 3, 92
Makura-no Soshi 188
Manjuji Temple.....................186
Manufacturing Industry...........218
Manyo-shu 185
Marunouchi 48
Mashu, Lake 13, 20
Mass-communication 67
Matsushima 29
Matsuda Gonroku 204
Matsui Joryu 204
Maya, Portrait of 183
Meiji government 201
Meiji Period....................201, 202
Meiji Shrine 51
Meiji, Emperor 51, 52, 76
Meishin Highway 104
Metropolitan Art Gallery 71
Metropolitan Police Office 48
Mikoshi 82
Minamotos, the, or
  Minamoto Family...............191
Minamoto-no Yoritomo... 25, 76, 85
Ministries 237
Miroku Bosatsu 192
Miso-soup or Misoshiru 229
Mito 39
Mito Mitsukuni 39
Mitsui Building 61
Miyako 29
Modern Literature Museum 71
Modern Sports 234
Mogami River 28
Momo-no Sekku 79
Momoyama 196
Moss Temple 120
Mugaku Sogen 192

245

Munakata Shiko 204
Munetaka Shinno 192
Muroji Temple 188
Muromachi Period 192
Museums in Tokyo 71
Muso Soseki 192

Nagasaki 164
Nagata-cho 48
Nagoya 109
Nakamise 55
Name of the Country 20
Nanzenji Temple 195
Nara 138
Nara Period 185
Narita-San Temple 40
National Diet Building 48, 238
National Holidays 77
National Museum of
  Modern Art 71
National Museum of
  Western Art 71
National Parks 97
National Science Museum.......... 71
National Stadium 50
National Theater 59, 62
New Tokaido Line.............. 45, 88
New Tokyo International
  Airport 40, 44
New Year's Day 79
Nicolai Cathedral 65
Nigatsu-doh 139
Nihon-shoki 185
Nihon, or Nippon 20
Nijo Castle 131
Nikko 36
Nikko-bosatsu 186
Nippon Theater 59
Nissei Theater 59
Noh 146
Nonomura Ninsei 200
Nori 229
Noto Peninsula 114
Noshiro 25
Nyoirin Kan-non 189

Obi 231
Obon or Urabon-e 81
Ocha-no-ma 233
Oda Nobunaga 196
Oeyama, Mt. 93
Oga Peninsula 30
Ogasawara Islands 92
Ogura Yuki 203
Oirase River 28

Oka Shikanosuke 203
Okazaki Park....................... 122
Okhotsk 19, 20, 21
Okinawa 92, 170
Okumura Dogyu.................... 203
O-kuni 146
Oku-no Hosomichi 33
Olympic Games 44
Ono-no Michikaze (Tofu) 189
Ooi River 107
Osorezan 28
Ota Dokan 76
Ou mountain range 25
Oyama 147
Oyashio 92

Pacific War 52, 76
Pearl 111
Perry, Commodore 197
Population......................... 3, 95
Publication 67

Religion 112
Rice 10, 229
Rikuchu 29
Rock-Garden 122, 133
Rokko, Mt. 154
Ryoanji Temple 122
Ryusen-do Cave 29

Sado 98
Sake 132, 154
Saihoji Temple 120
Saikai Bridge 167
Sakaida Kakiemon 200
Sakamoto Hanjiro 203
Sakurajima 170
Sakyamuni 134
Samurai 134
Sangatsu-doh 139
Sansui-ga 28, 191
Sapporo 16
Sapporo Snow Festival 17
Sarugaku 146
Sasebo 167
Sashimi 229
Sato Gengen 204
Sawa-chidori Makie 189
Seiryoden 131
Sendai 29
Sen-no Rikyu...................... 98
Senri Kyuryo 151
Sensoji Temple 53, 55
Setomono 109
Setsubun 79

246

Shaka Sanzon 183
Shibuya 53
Shichi-Go-San 81
Shigure-tei 197
Shindenzukuri 132
Shinjuku 53
Shinjuku Gardens 51
Shikoku 157, 159
Shimizu Nanzan 204
Shimokita Peninsula 28
Shimomura Kanzan 202
Shintoism 110, 112, 115
Shippoyaki 109
Shishinden 131
Shitenno 189
Shitsu Kongoshin 185
Shizuoka 106
Shogatsu 79
Shogun 76
Shogunate Government 85, 191
Sho-in (zukuri) 195
Shotoku, Prince 138
Shugaku-in Imperial Villa 200
Smock frock 30
Soba 230
Sokokuji Temple 195
Sports 234
Sugiyama Yasushi 203
Suigo 40
Sukiyaki 230
Sukiya-zukuri 9
Sumi 103
Sumida River..........................67
Sumo 234
Suzuri 103
Suzuki Suiken 204

Tairas, the, or Taira Clan ... 85, 191
Taisho Period 201, 202
Tama cemetery 81, 83
Tanabata 26
Tango-no Sekku 79
Tatami 233
Tazawa, Lake 28
Tea Ceremony ... 99, 134, 196, 197
Television 67, 223
Temmangu Shrine......................83
Tempura 230
Tenpyo Culture 185
Toba 111
Toba, the bishop 189
Todaiji Temple 138
Tofu 229
Tofukuji Temple 195
Toji Temple 123

Tohoku New Trunk Line 25
Toko-no-ma 101
Tokugawas, the 197
  (cf. Bakufu, Shogun, Shogunate
   Government, Edo)
Tokugawa Ieyasu.. 76, 106,151, 197
Tokugawa Period.............. 76, 197
Tokuoka Shinsen 203
Tokyo Bay 60
Tokyo Central Wholesale
  Market 65
Tokyo Monorail 60
Tokyo National Museum 71
Tokyo St. Mary Cathedral 65
Tokyo Tower 47
Tone River 40
Torii 52
Torii Kiyonobu 201
Toshogu Shrine 36
Toyama 114
Toyotomi Hideyoshi 127, 196
Towada, Lake 28
Tsuchigumo-soshi 195
Tsukiji Honganji Temple.............65
Typhoon 24

University of Tokyo 69
Umehara Ryuzaburo 203
Uno Sesson 204
Uo Ichiba 65
Usorizan, Lake 28
Uwajima 10

Waka 33, 185
Wakato Great Bridge 170
Wakita Kazu 203
Waseda University 69
World War I 202
World War II 202, 213, 219

Yagisawa dam 38
Yakushi-nyorai 183
Yamaboko 117
Yamaguchi Hoshun 203
Yamamoto Kyujin 203
Yamashita Park 84
Yamate (Belt) Line............... 45, 49
Yamato-e 195
Yasaka Shrine 132
Yasuda Yukihiko 203
Yasukuni Shrine 52
Yayoi wares..................... 179, 182
Yodogawa River 151
Yokkaichi 110

247

Yokohama 84
Yokote Basin 30
Yokoyama Taikan 202
Yokozuna 234
Yomeimon 36, 37
Yukata 11
Yukio Endo 236
Yumedono Chapel 141

Yuzawa 30

Zao, Mt. 31
Za-zen 134
Zen Buddhism................. 134, 191
Zen-Buddhist Temples......... 85, 191
Zuiganji Temple 29